# Amazing Coloring book
## Animals mandala
## for adult

COPYRIGHT 2020

ALL RIGHT RESERVED

the content contained within this book
may not be reproduced, duplicated,
Or transmitted without direct
written permission from the author
or the copyright owner.

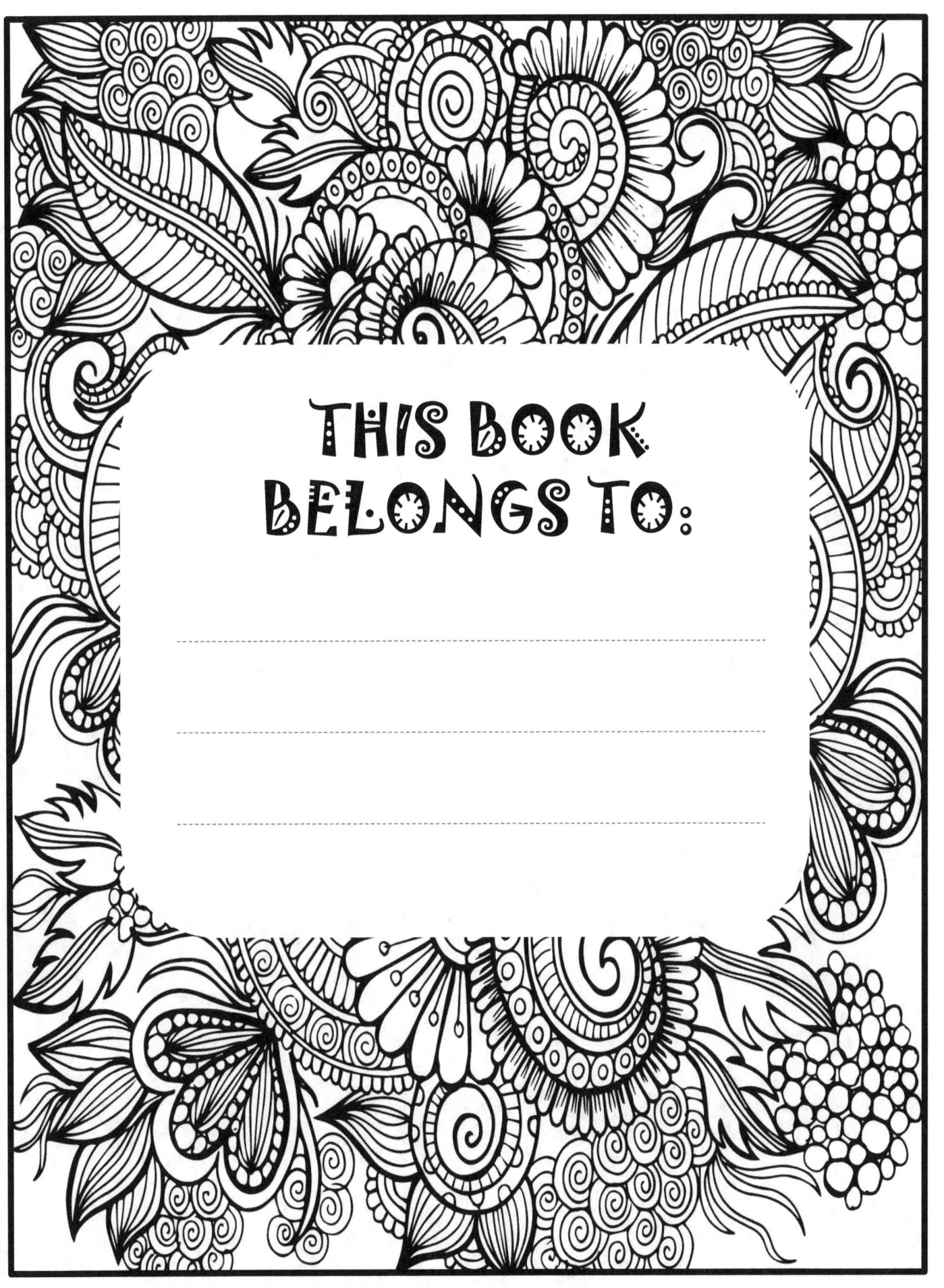

# Color Test Page

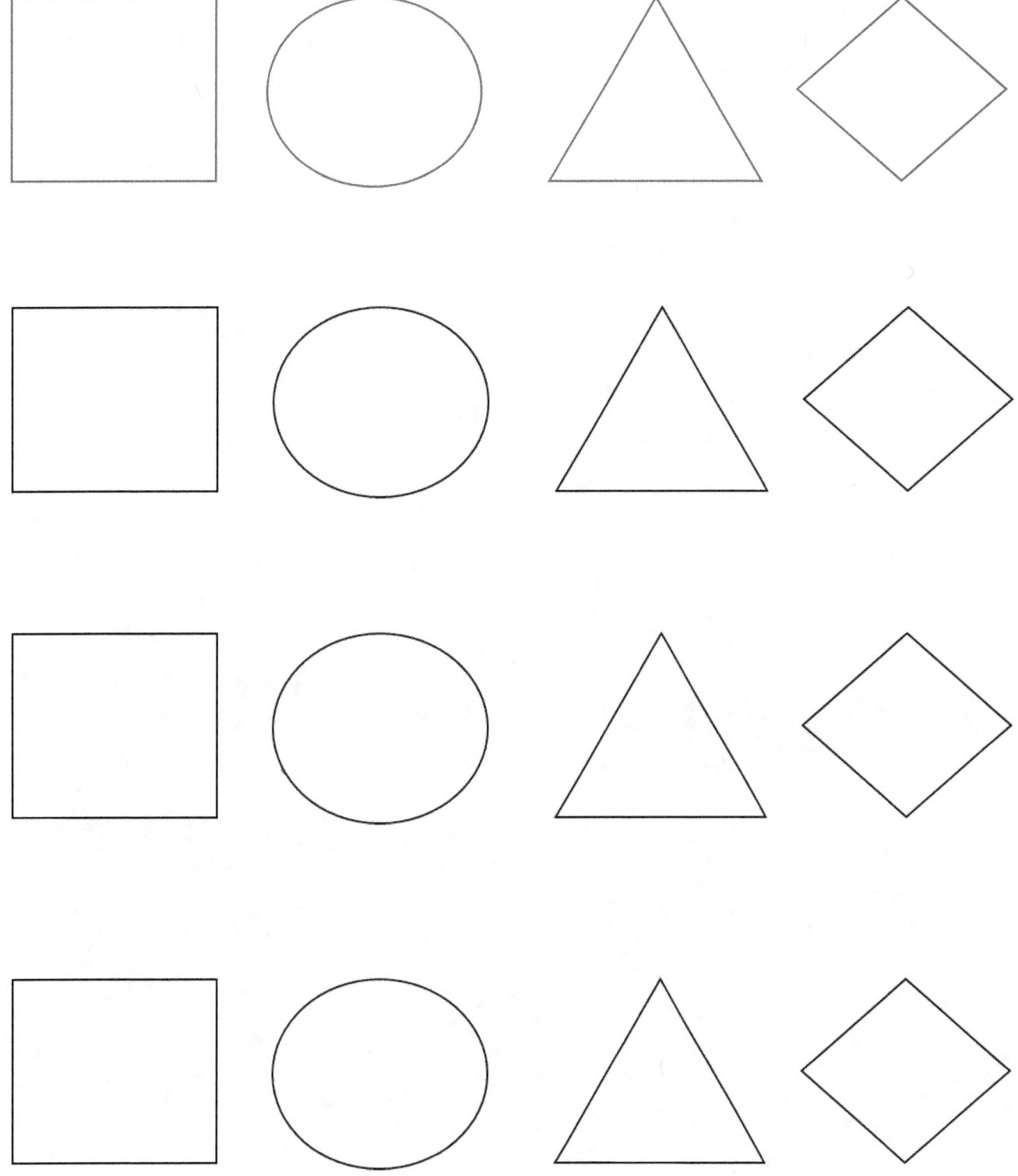

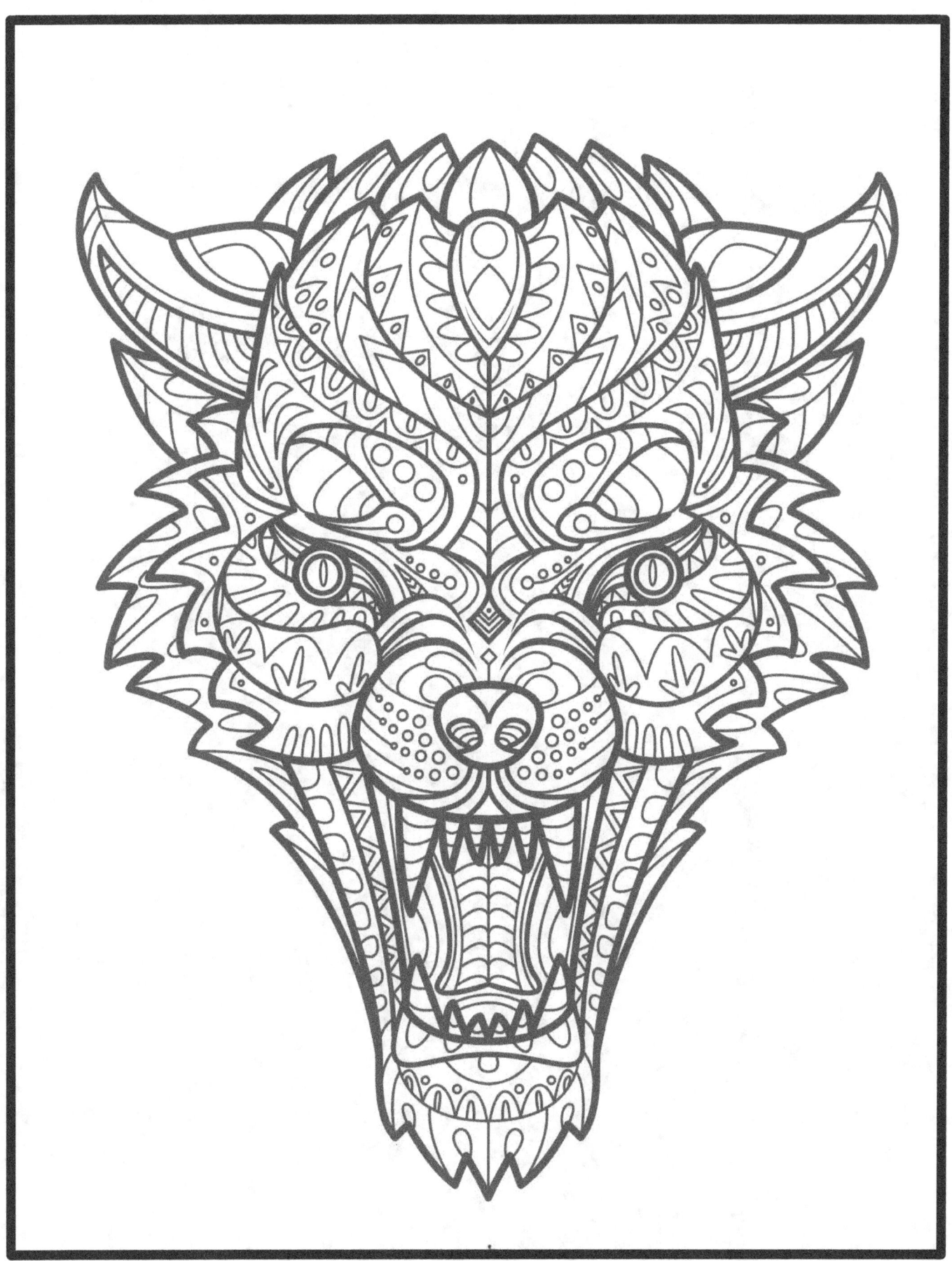

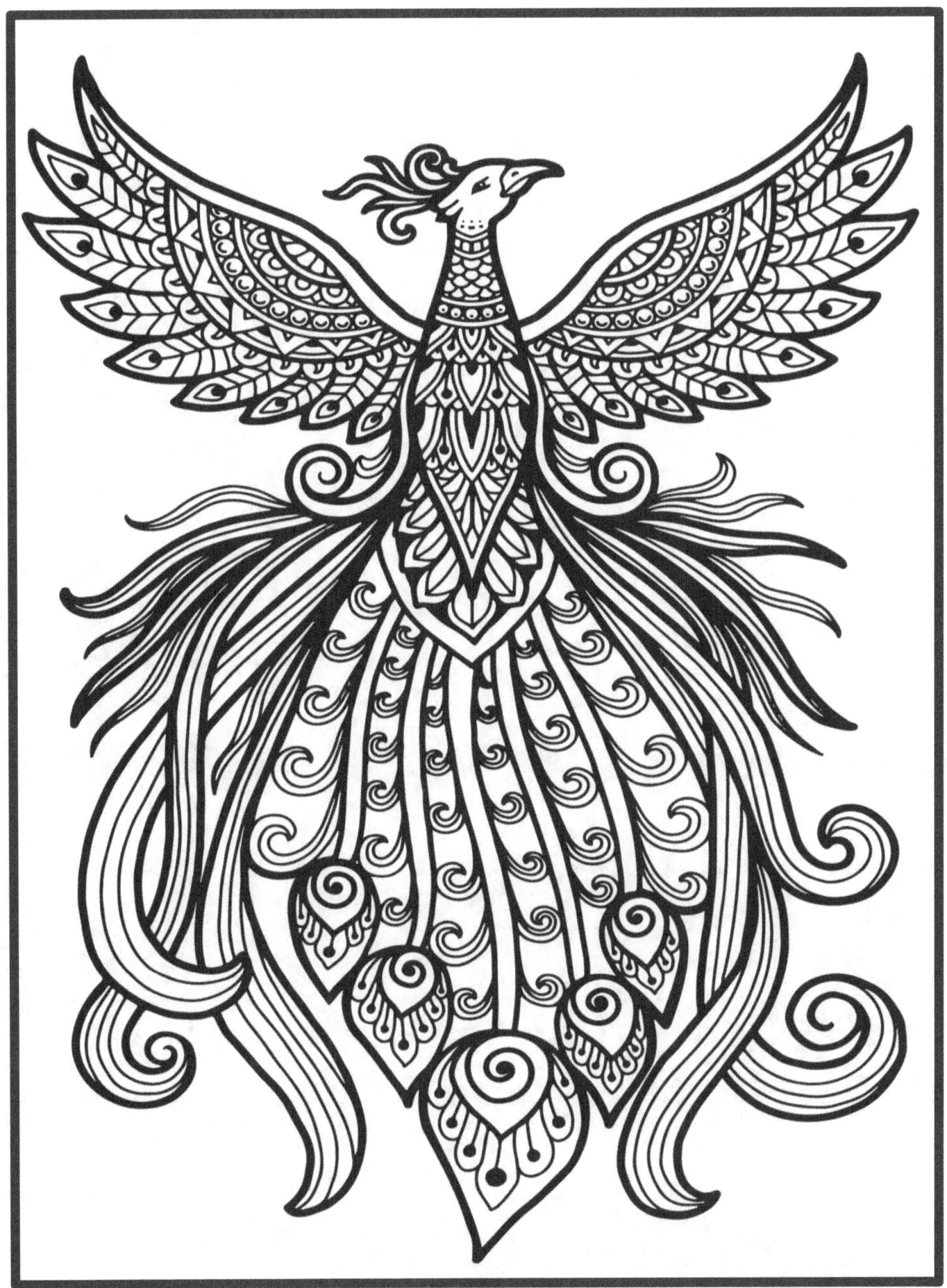

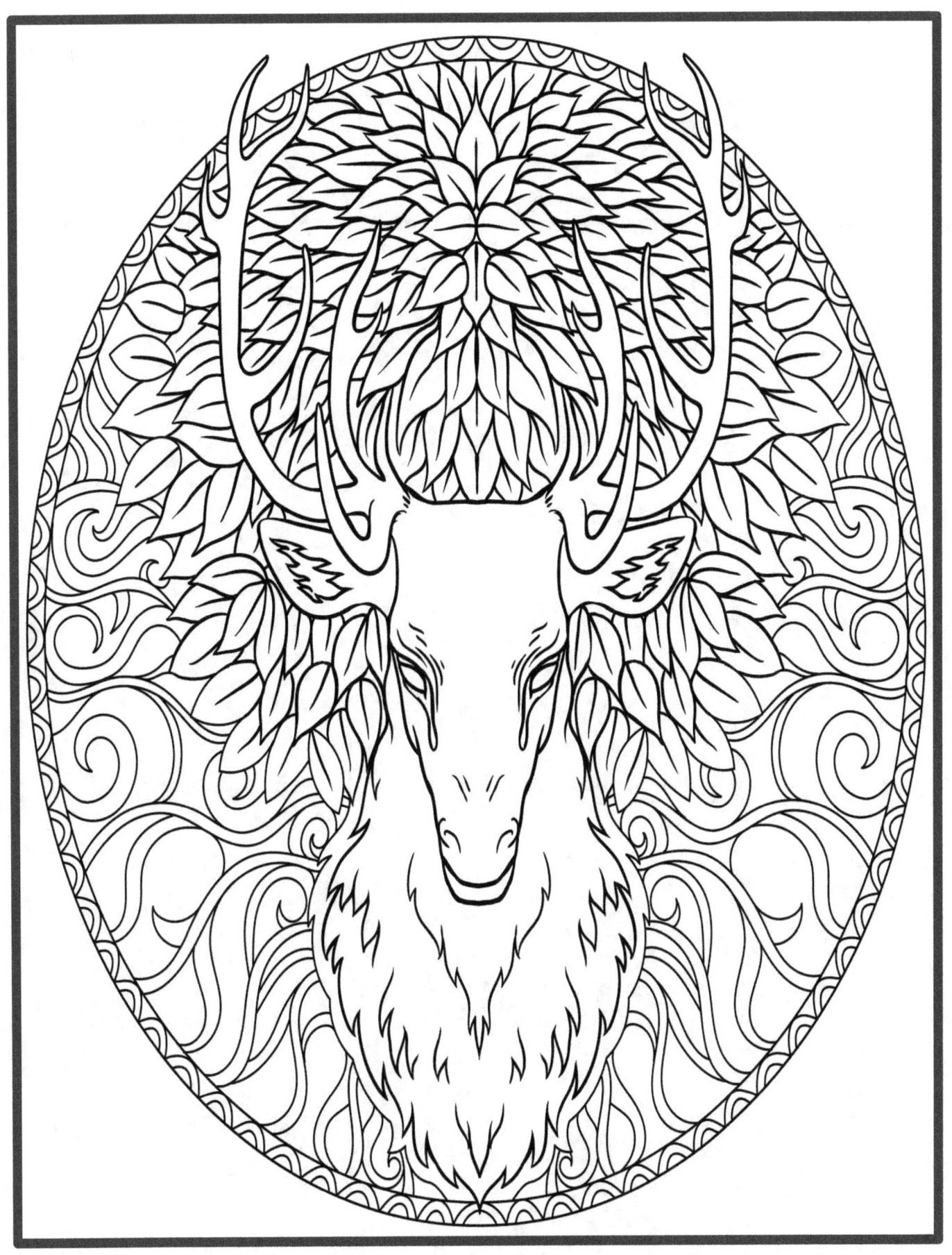

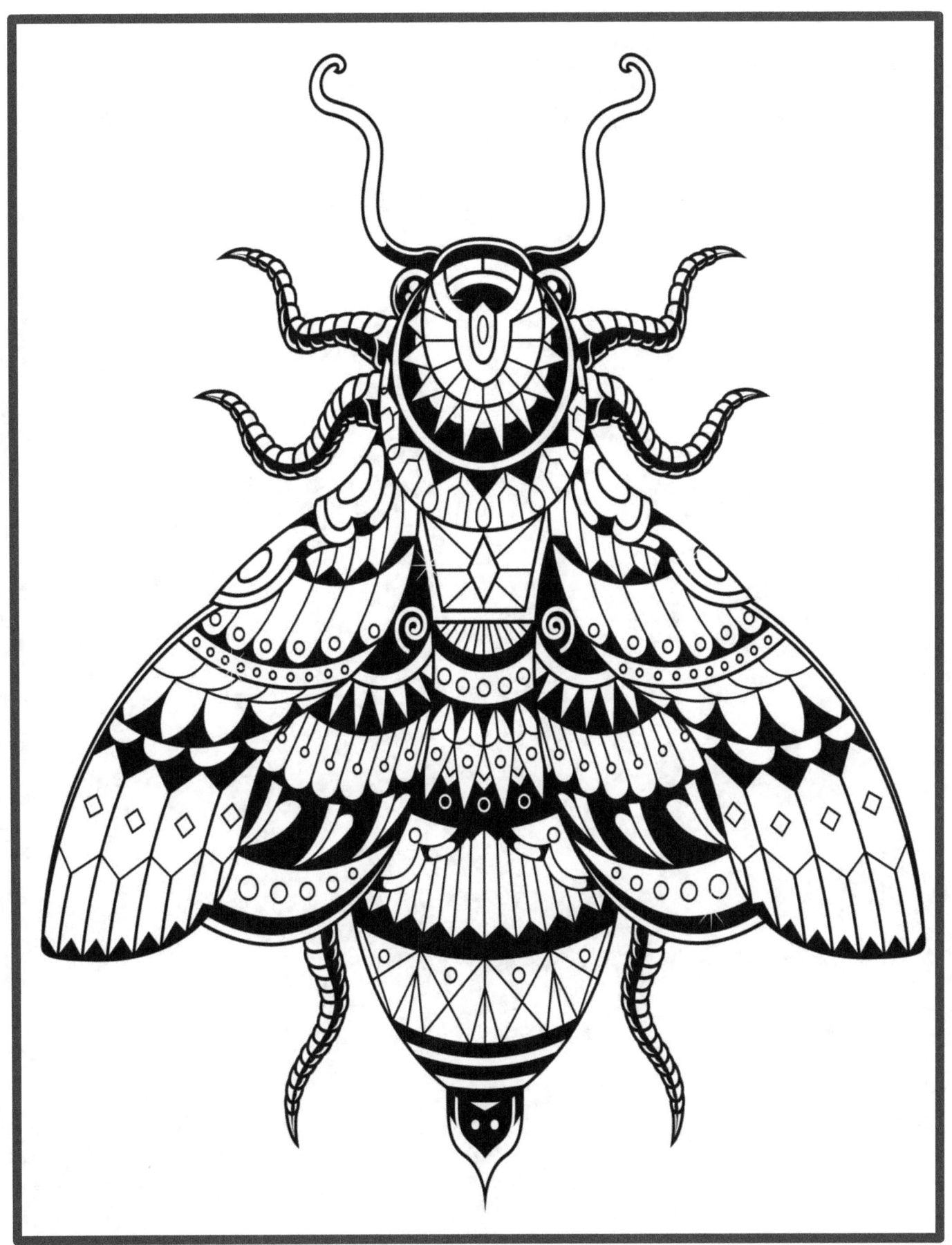

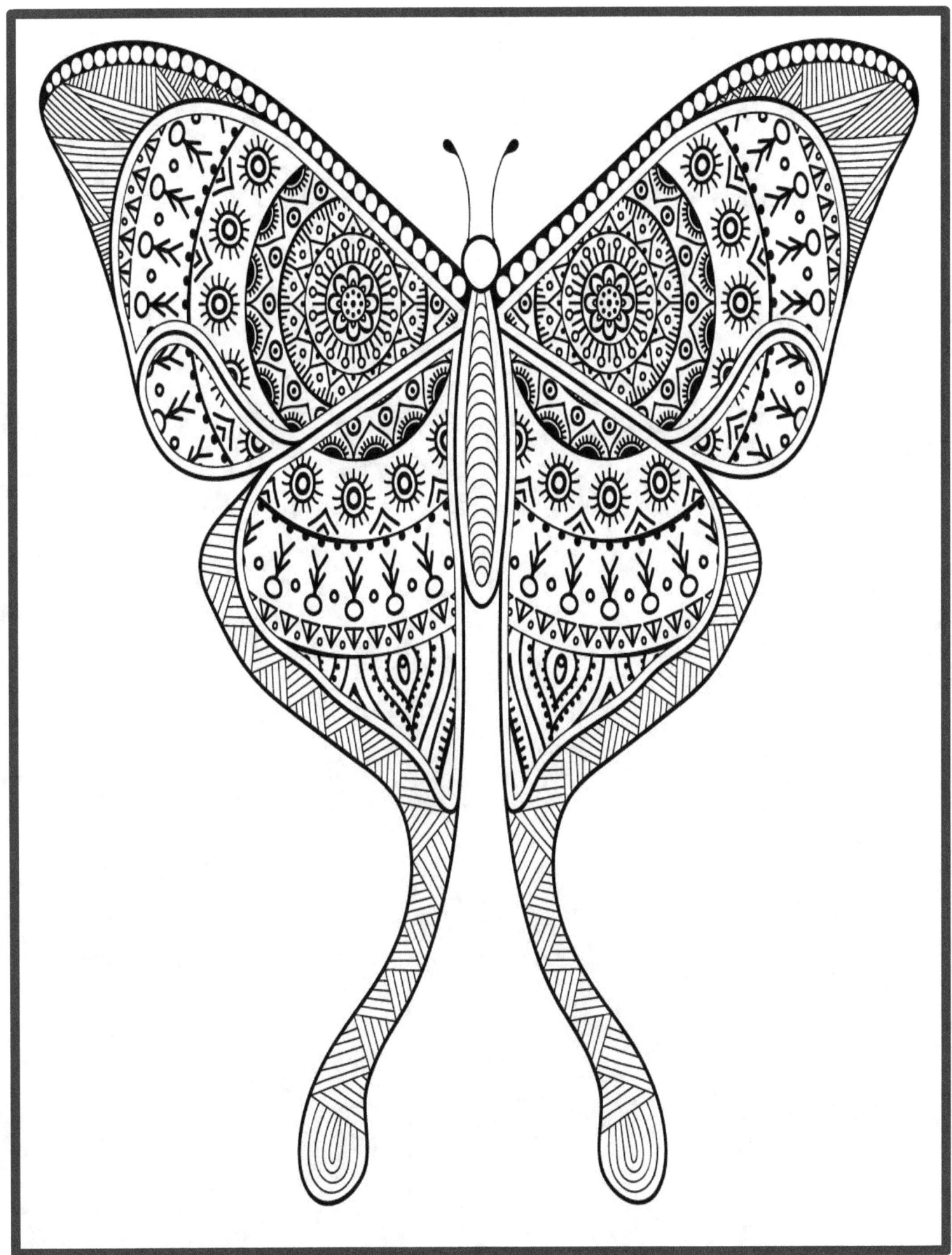

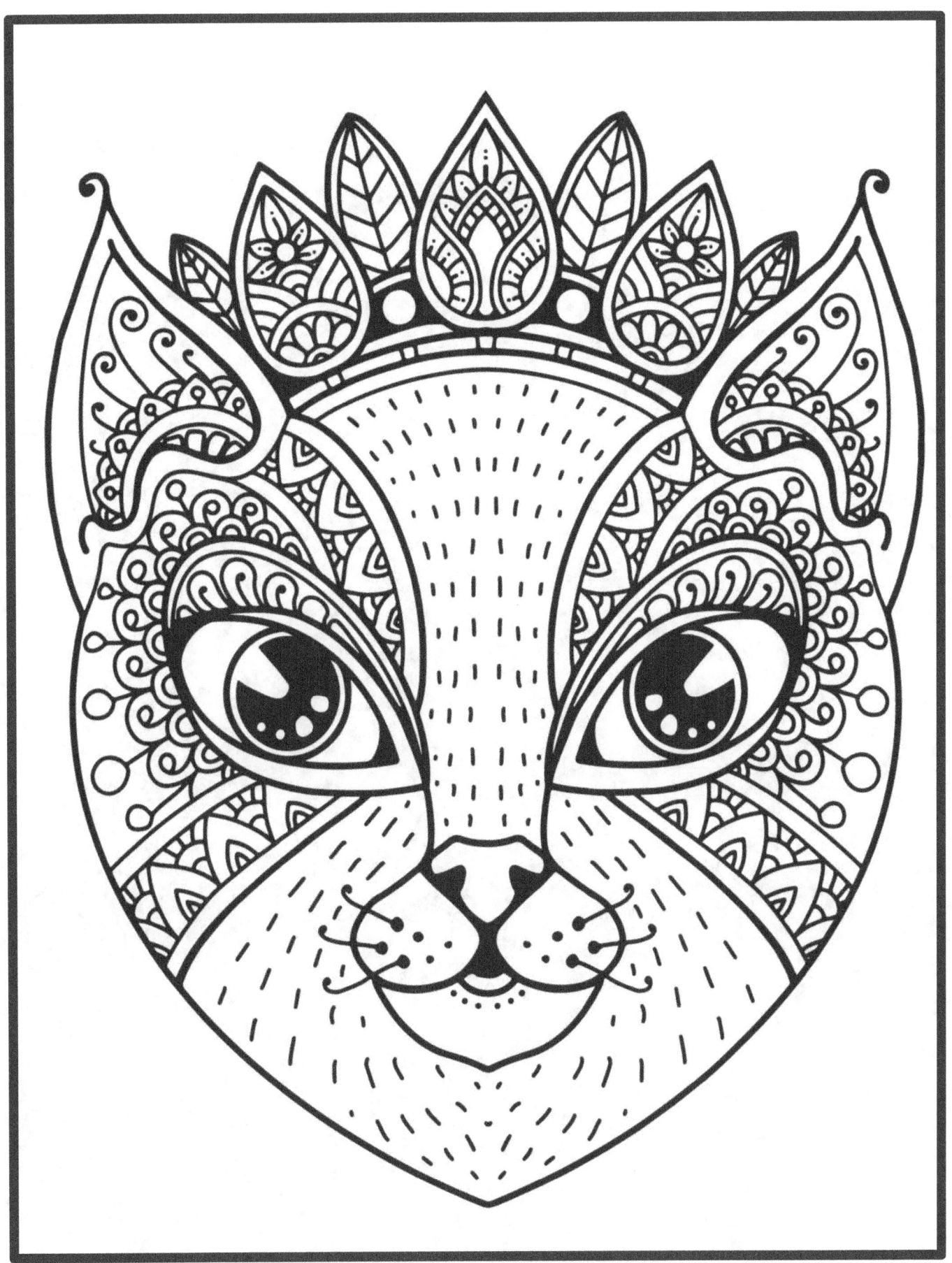

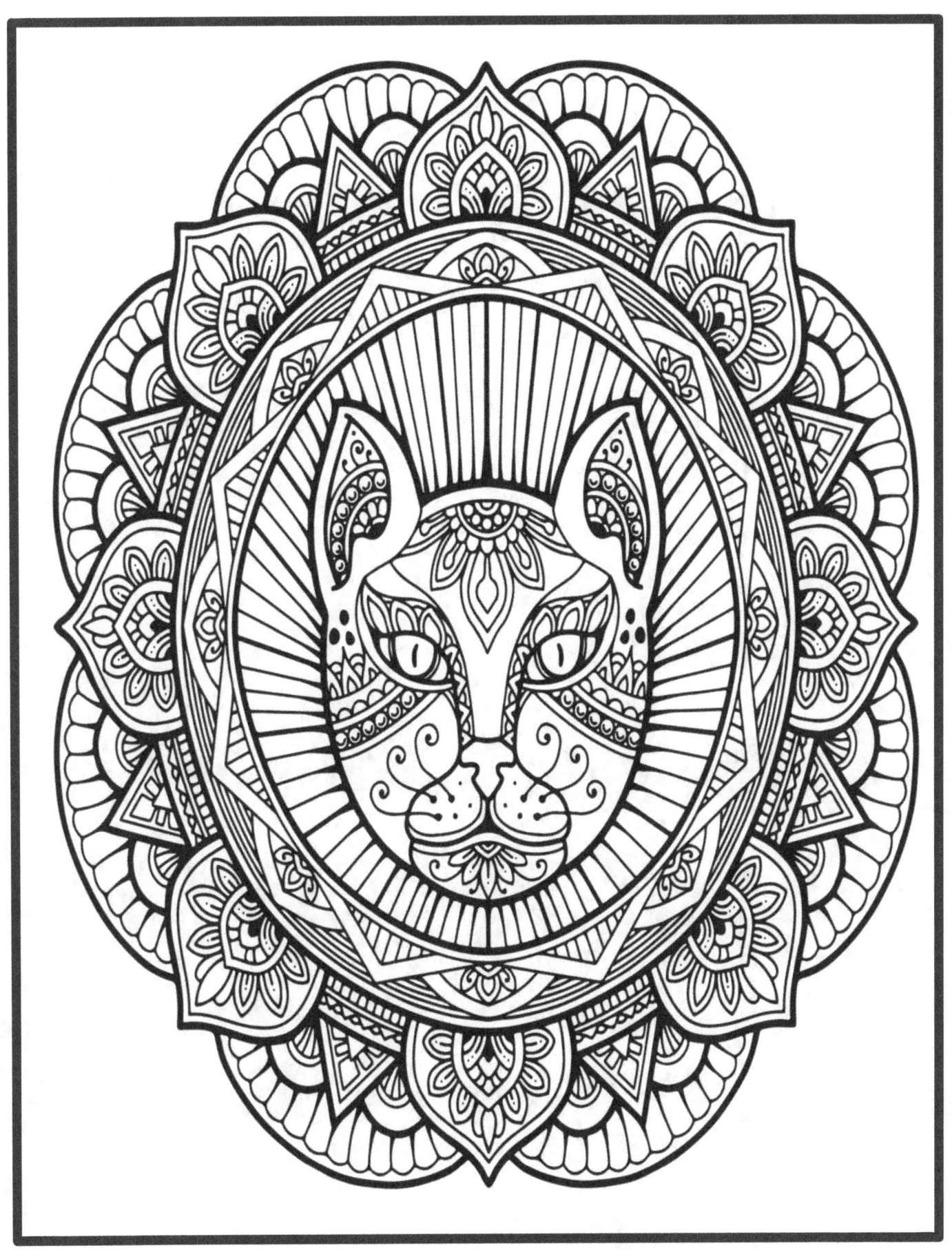

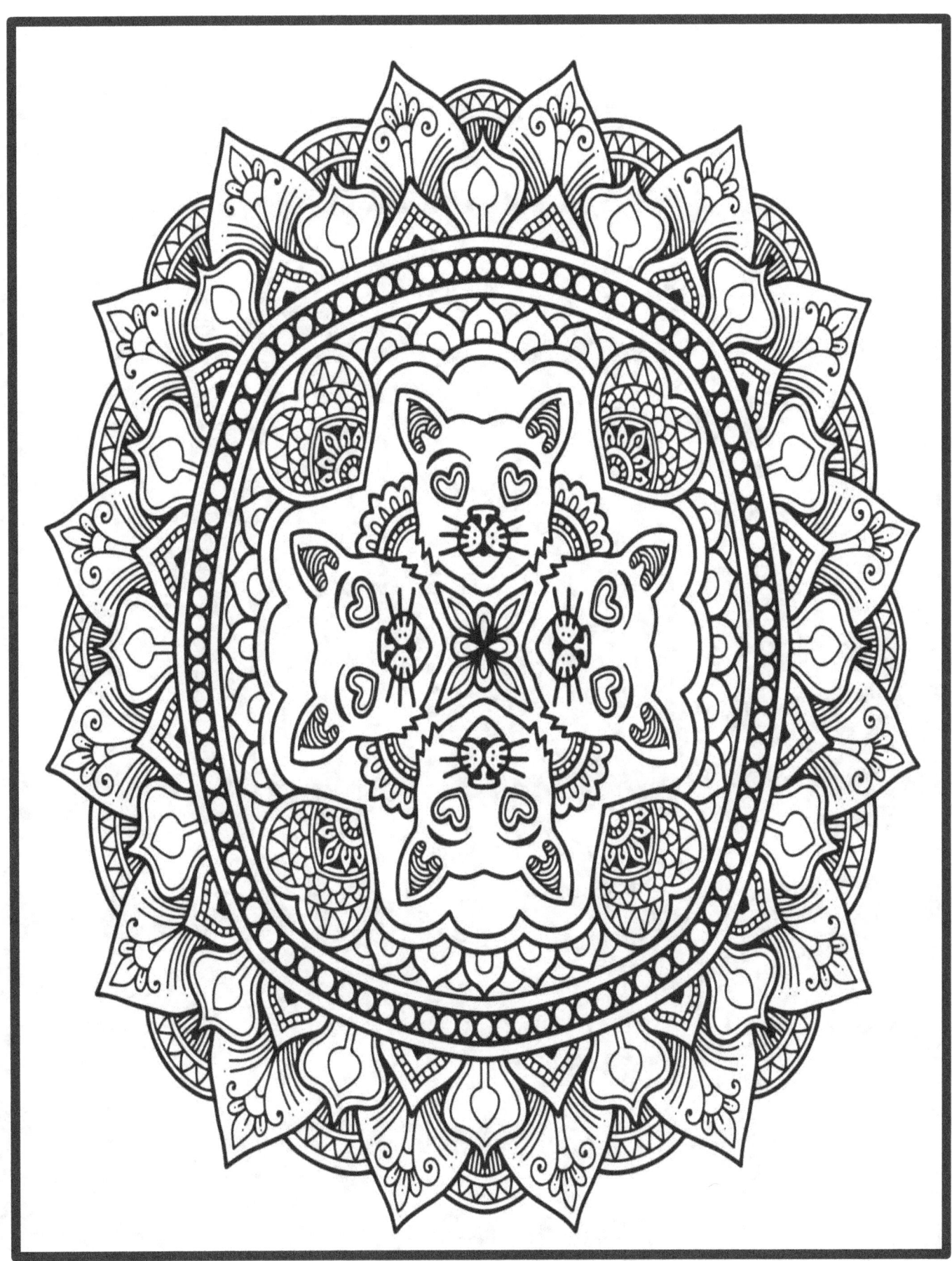

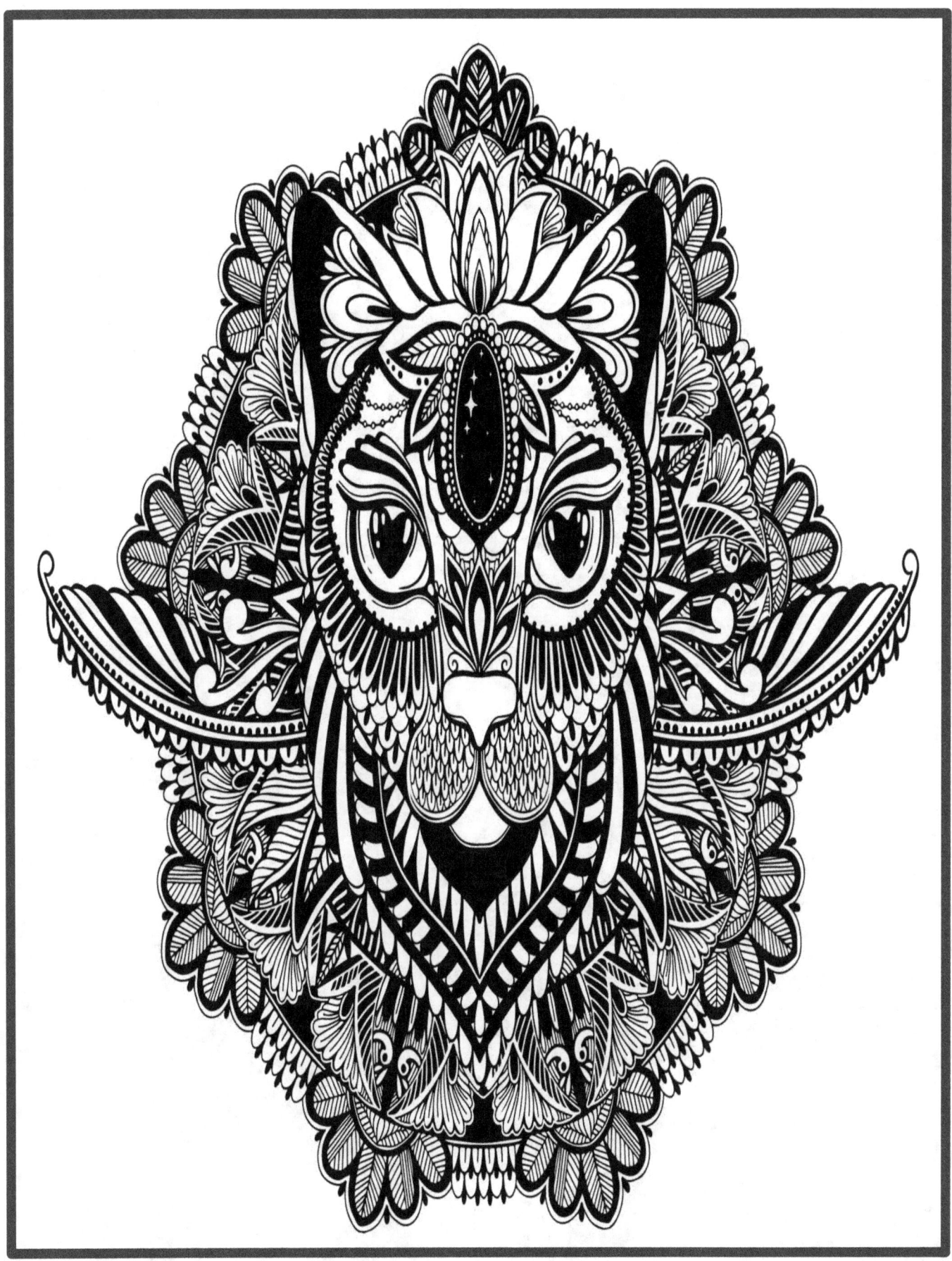

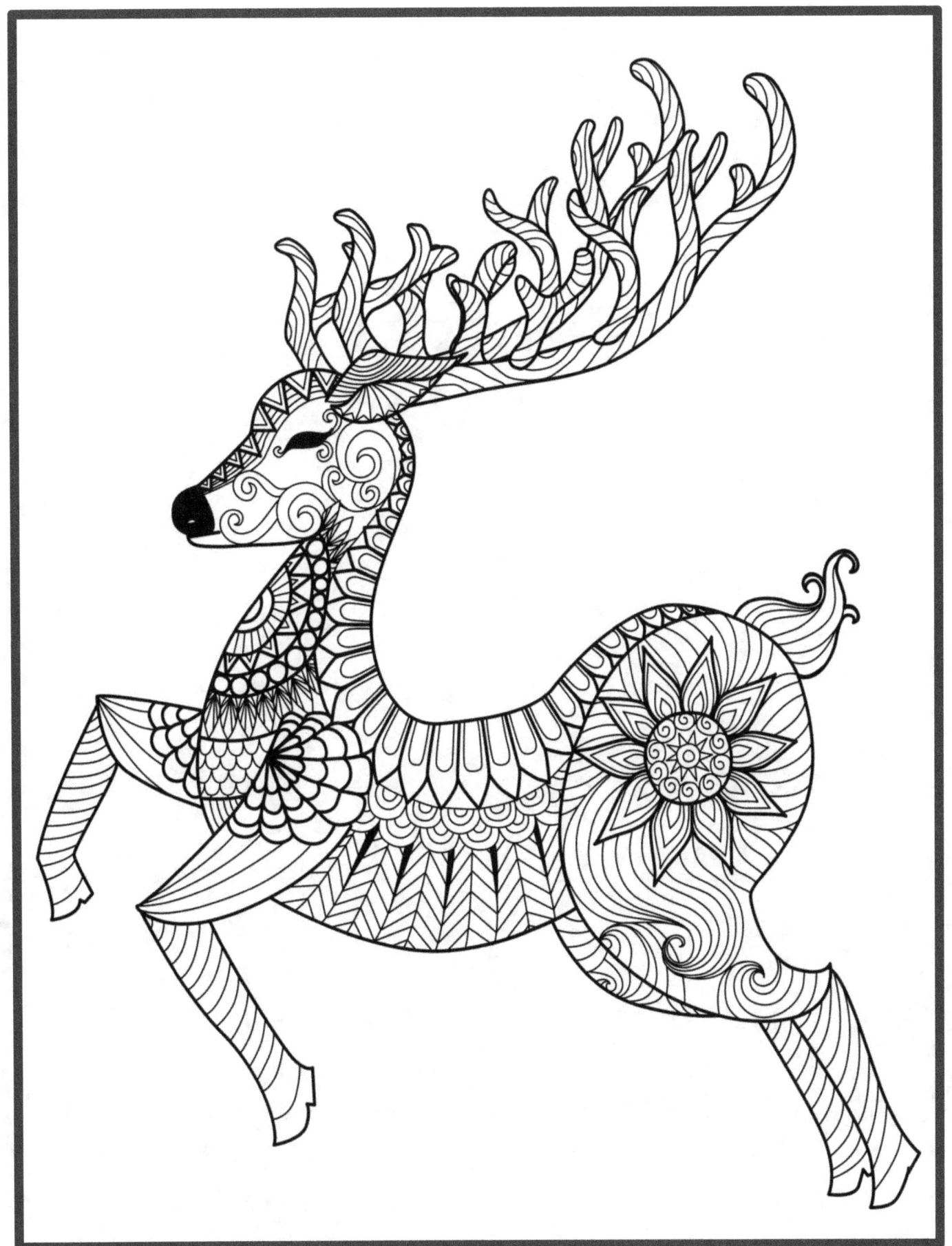

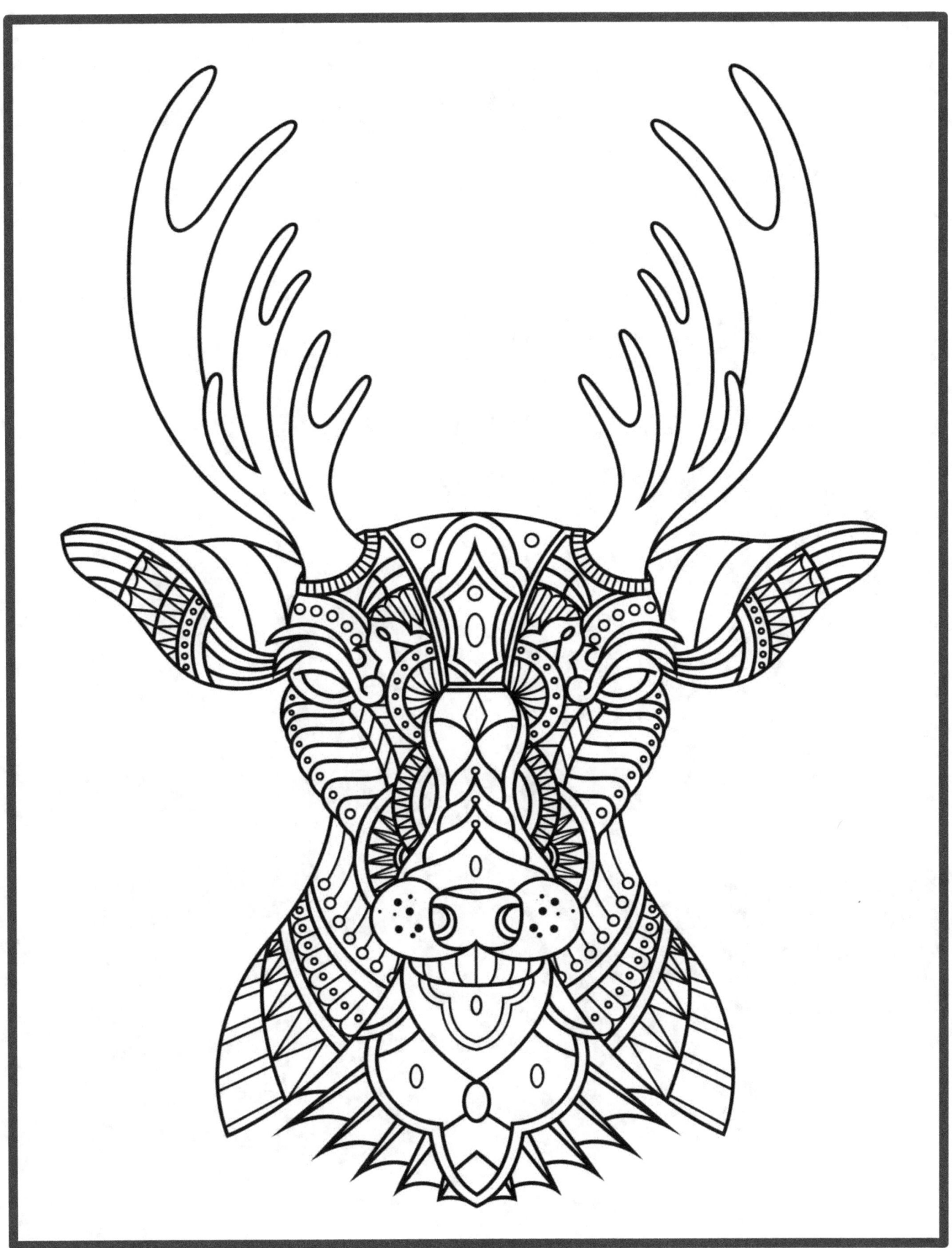

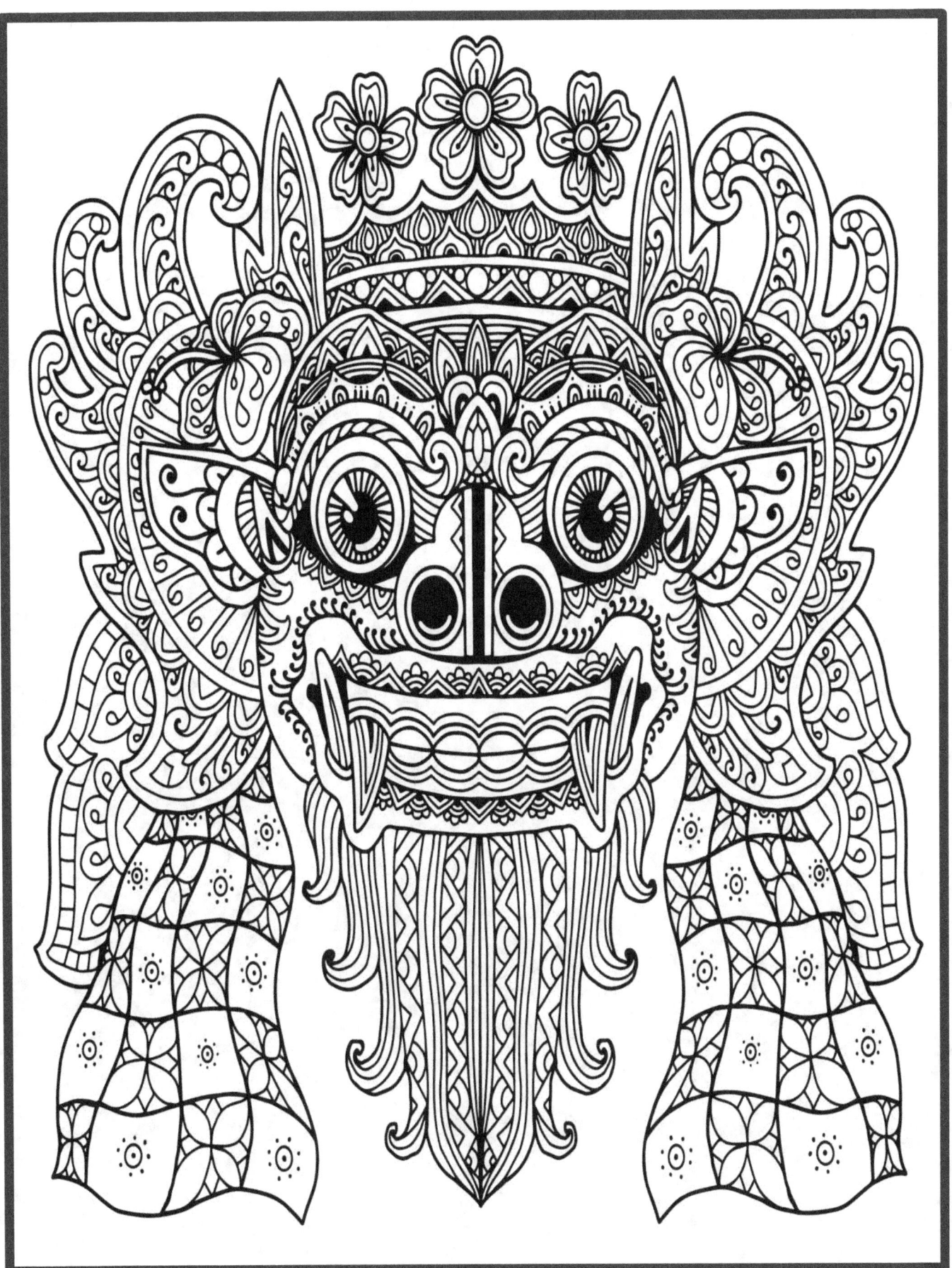

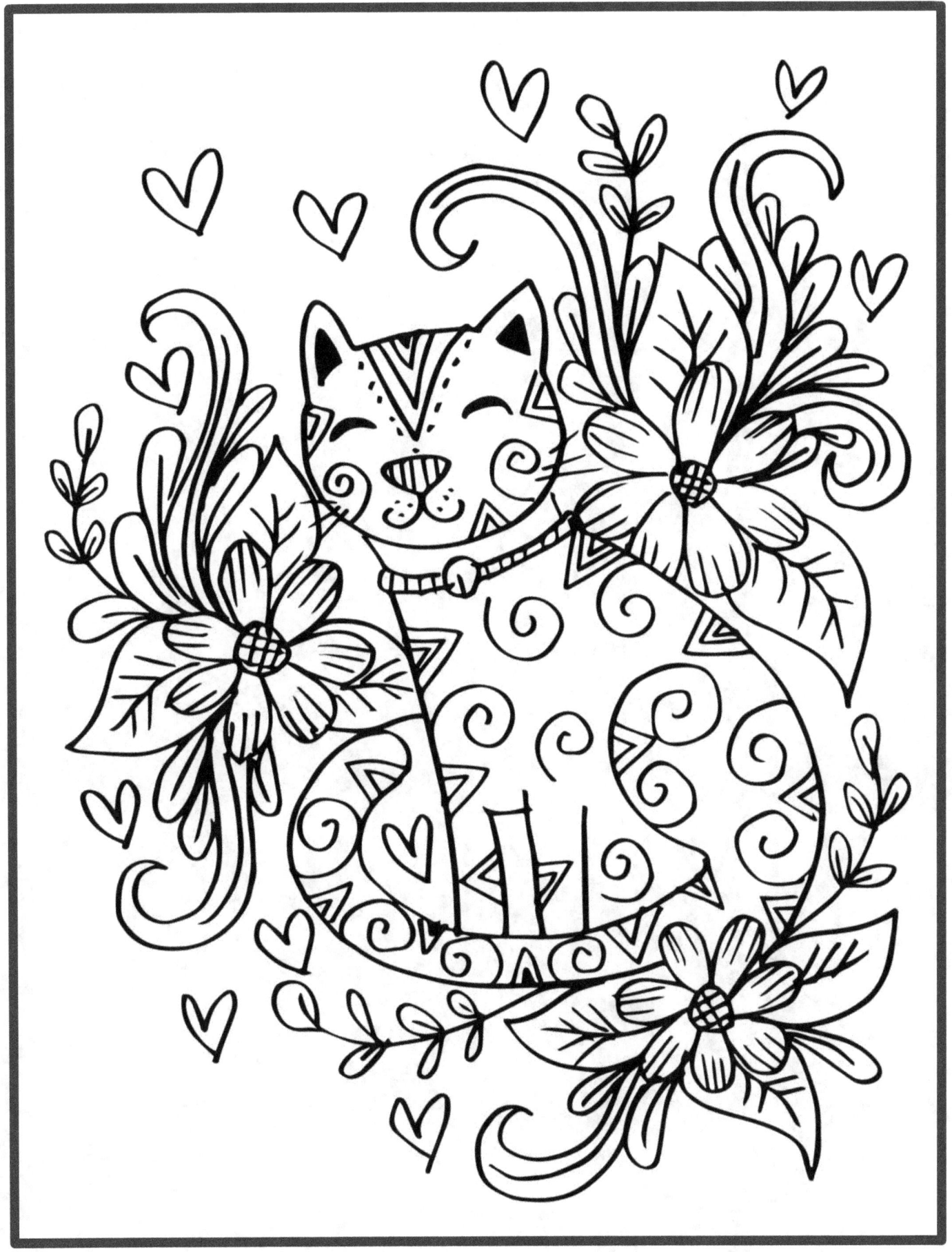

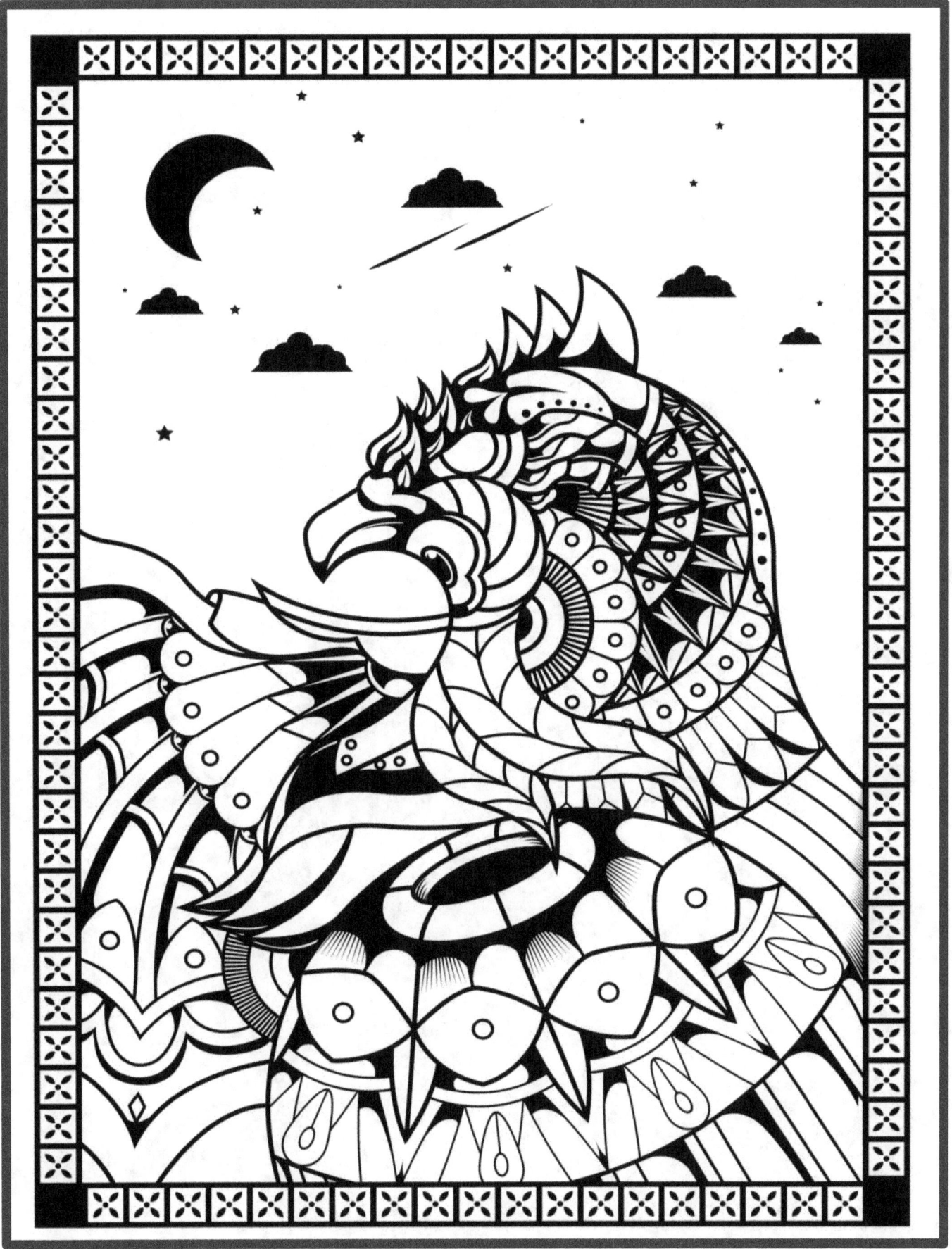

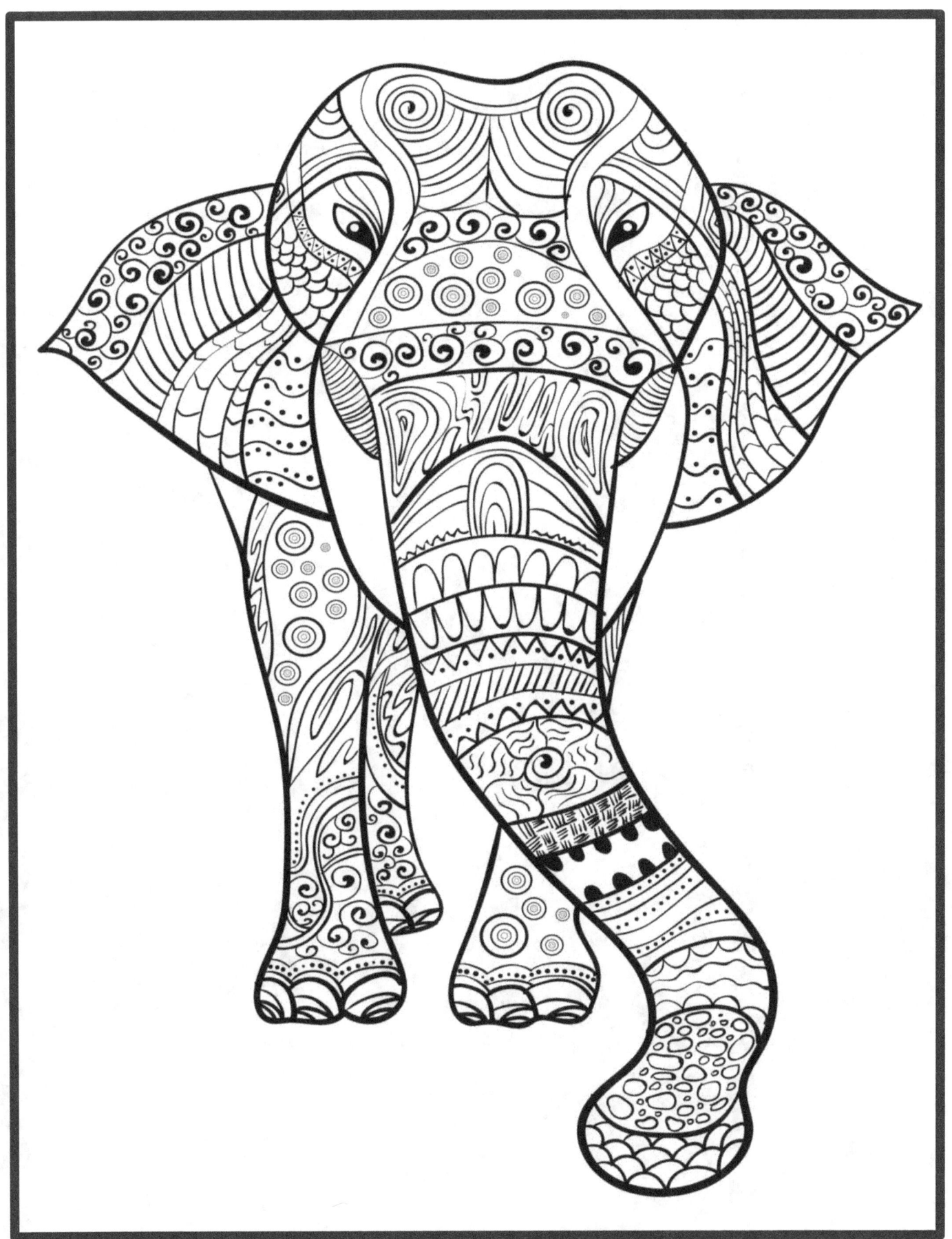

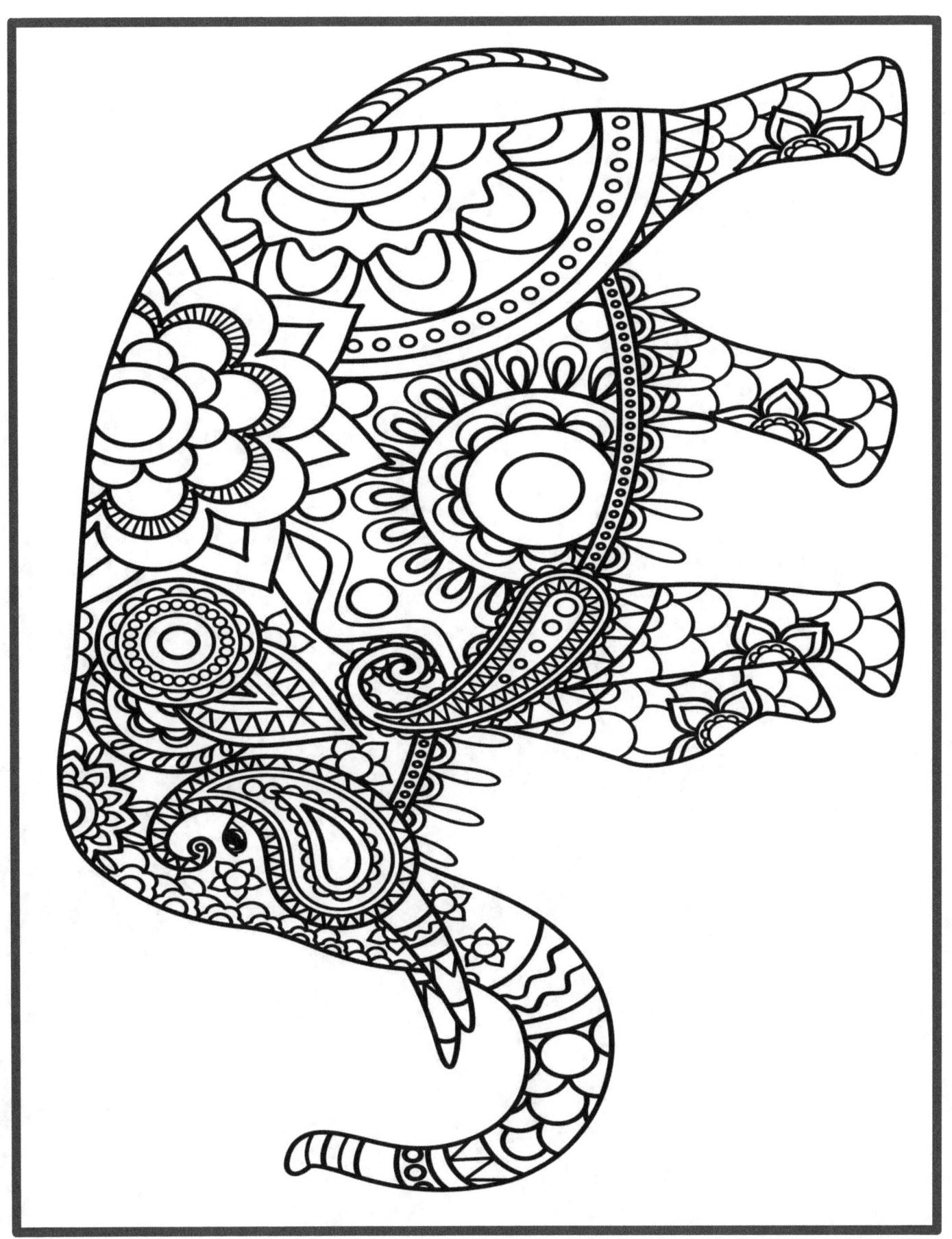

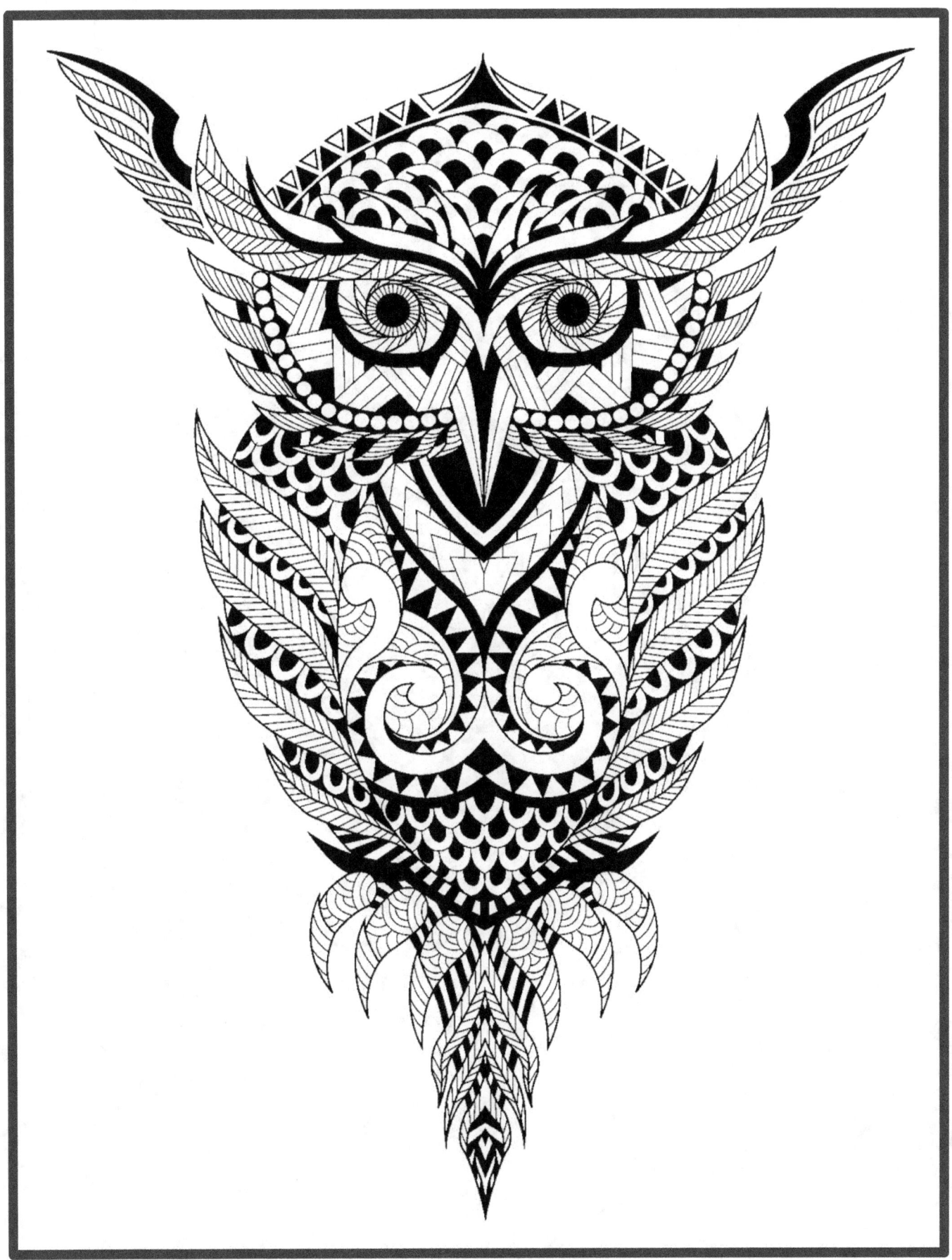

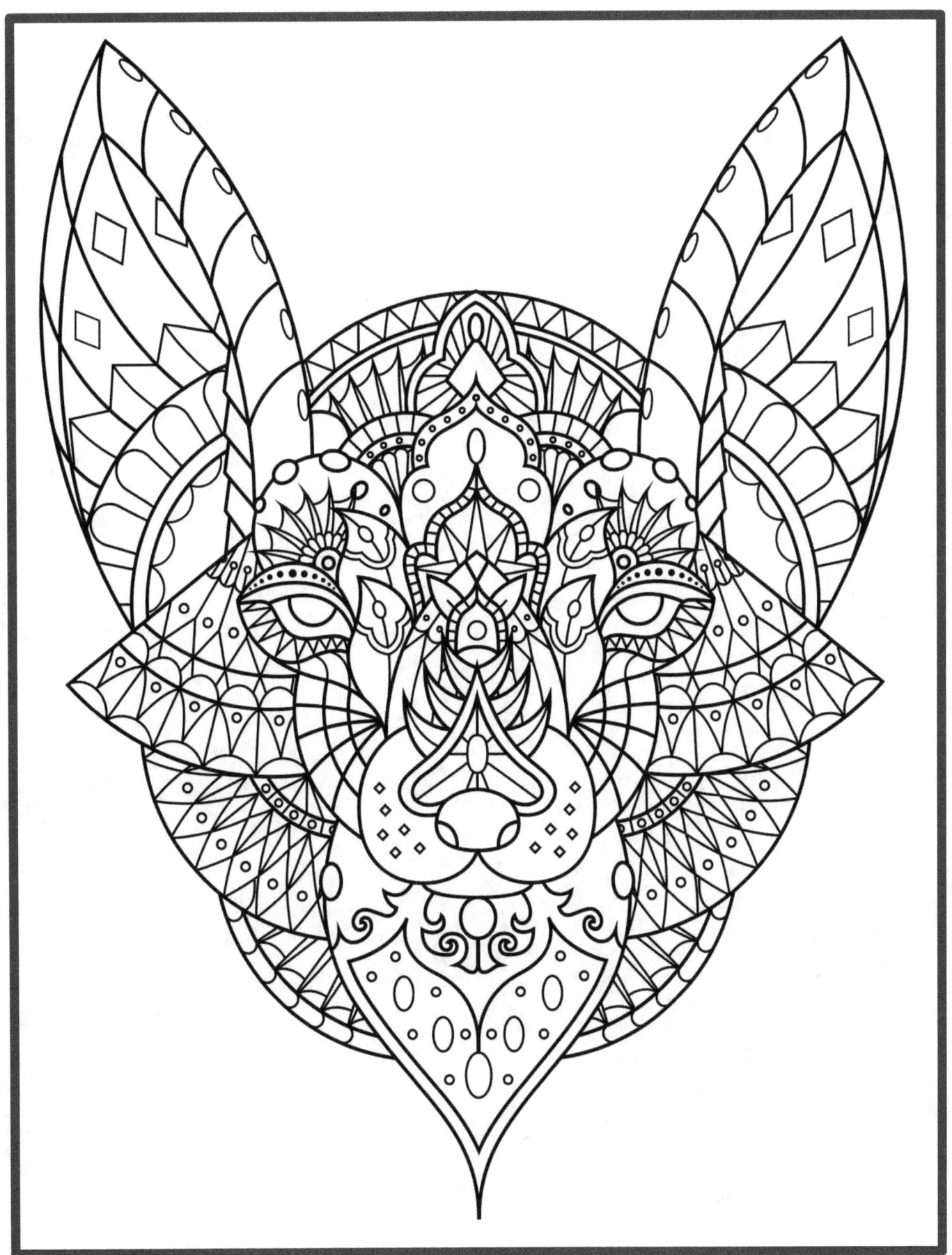

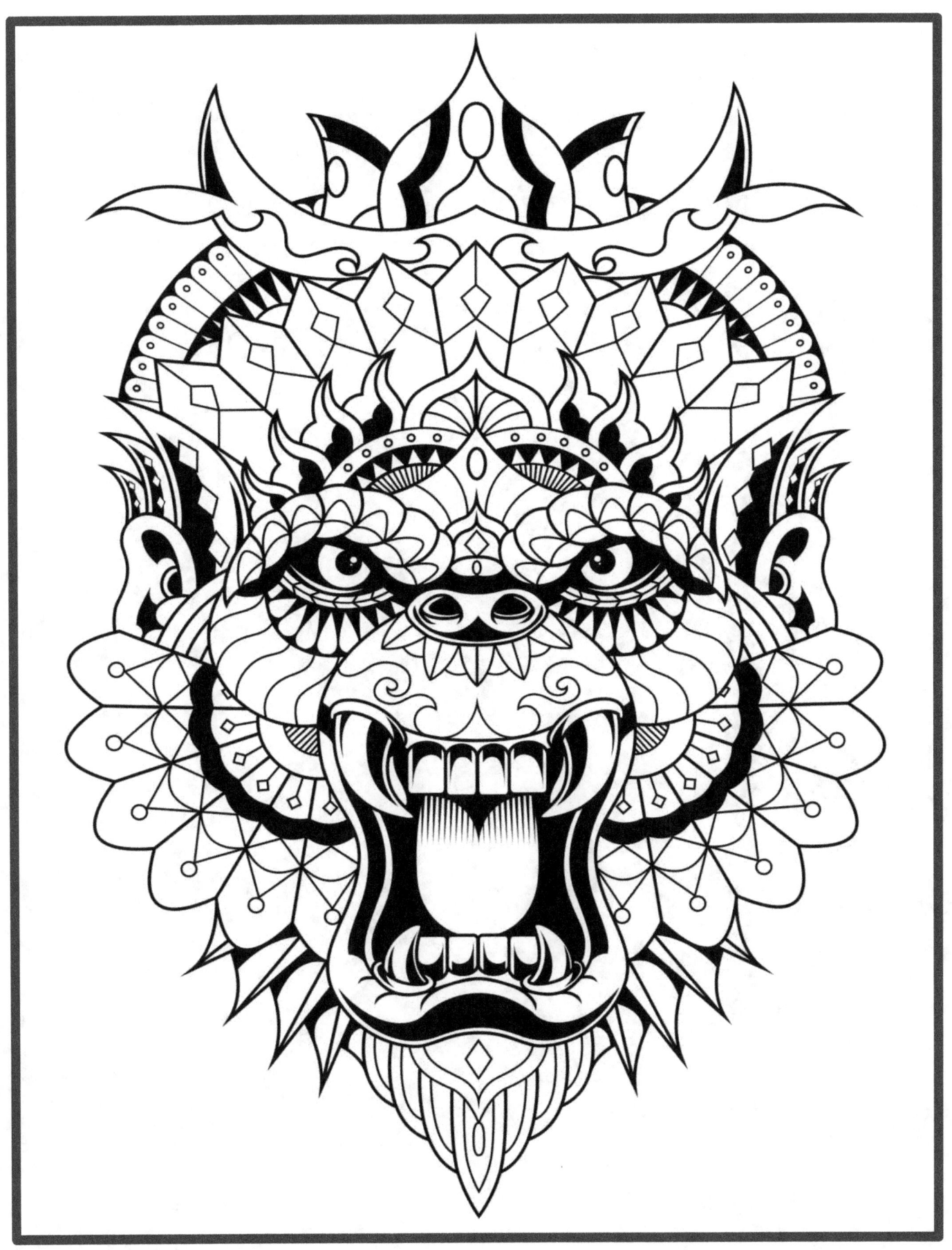

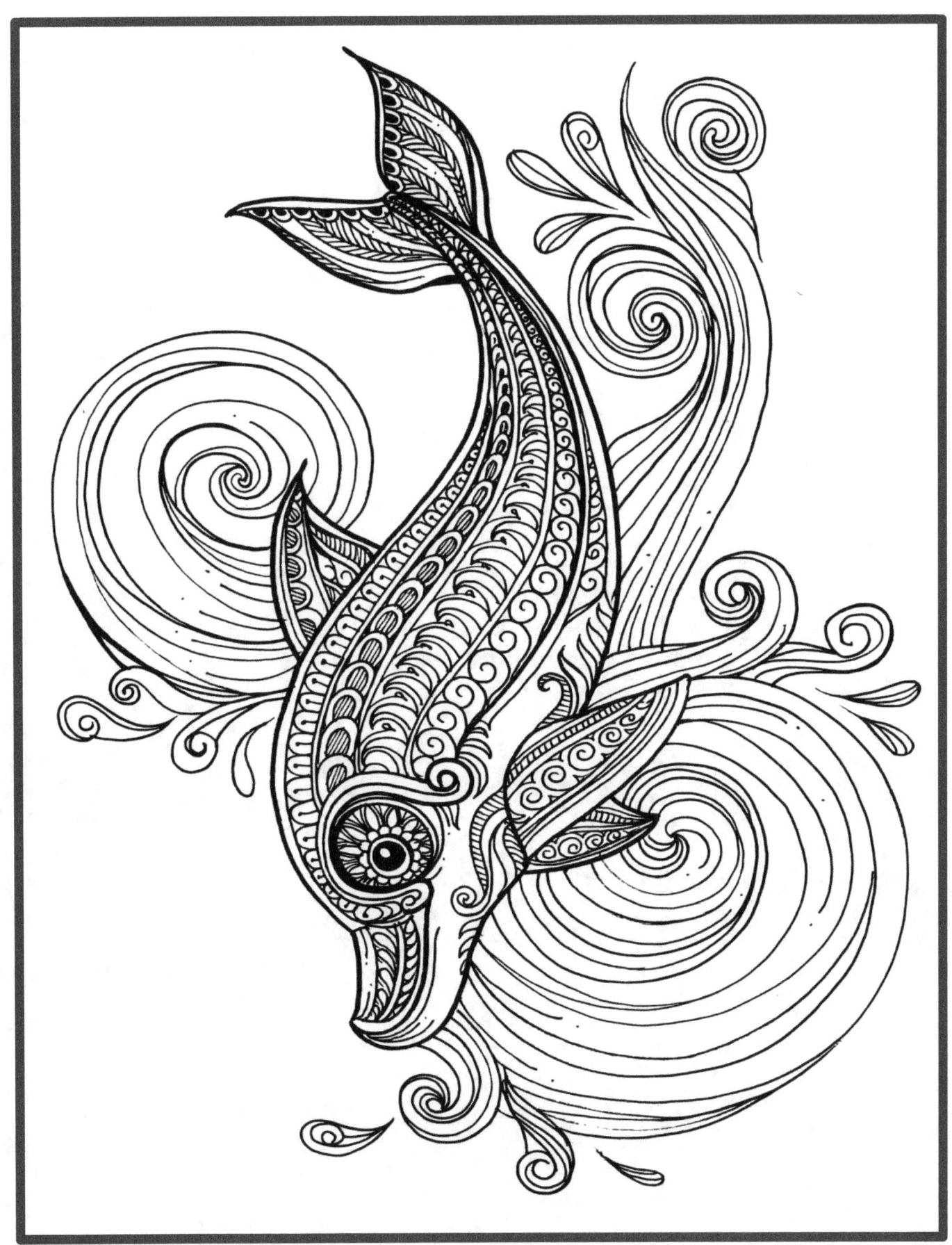

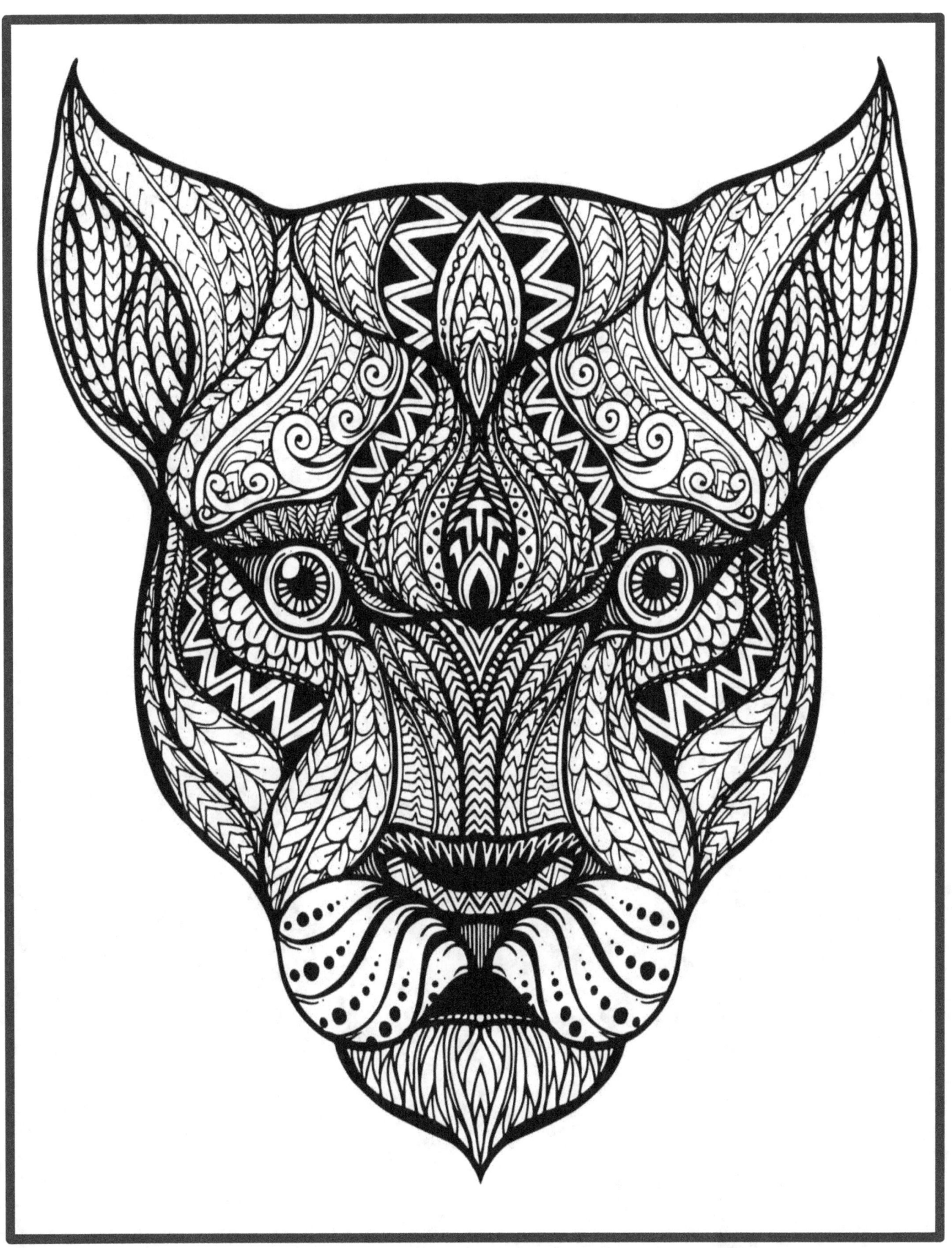

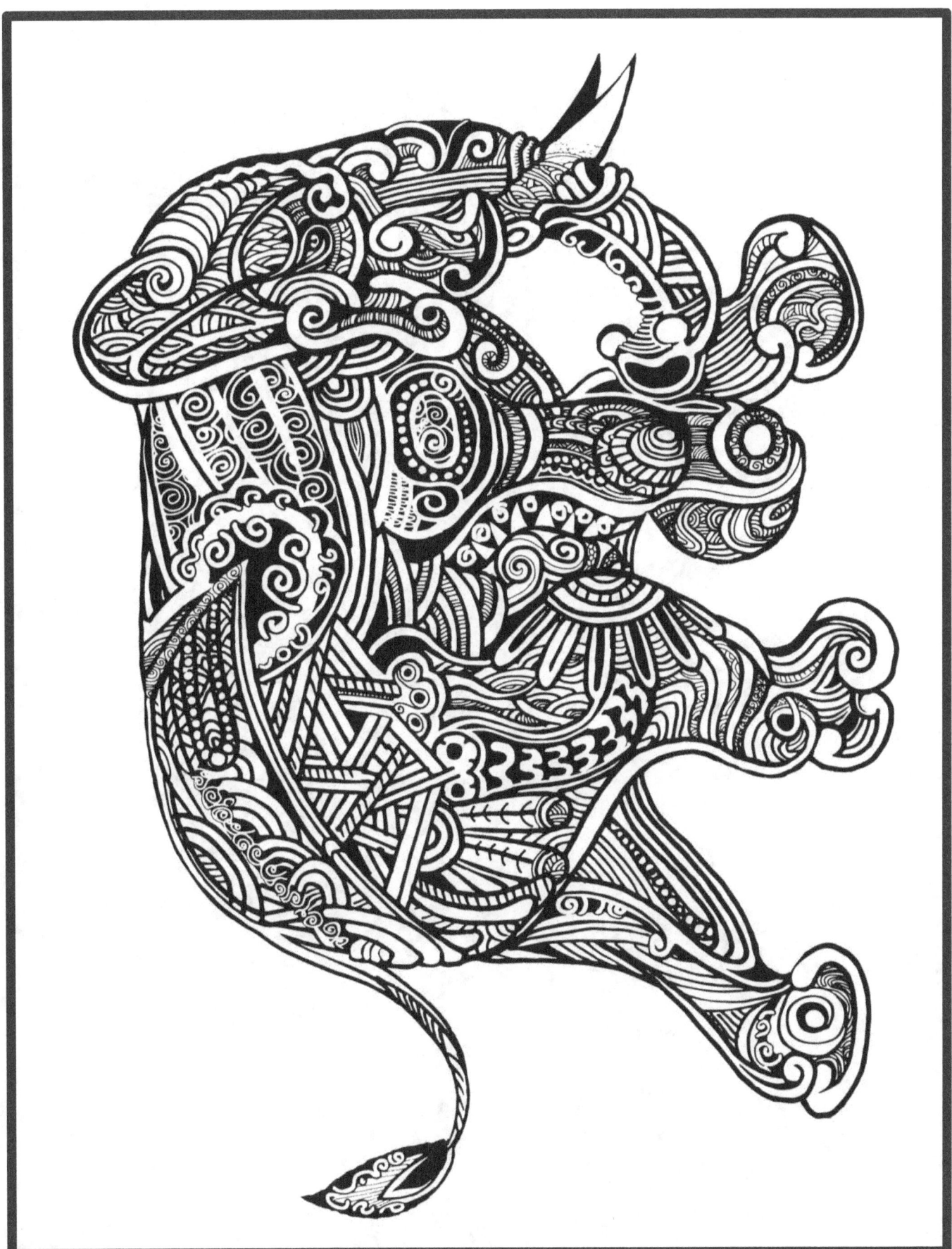

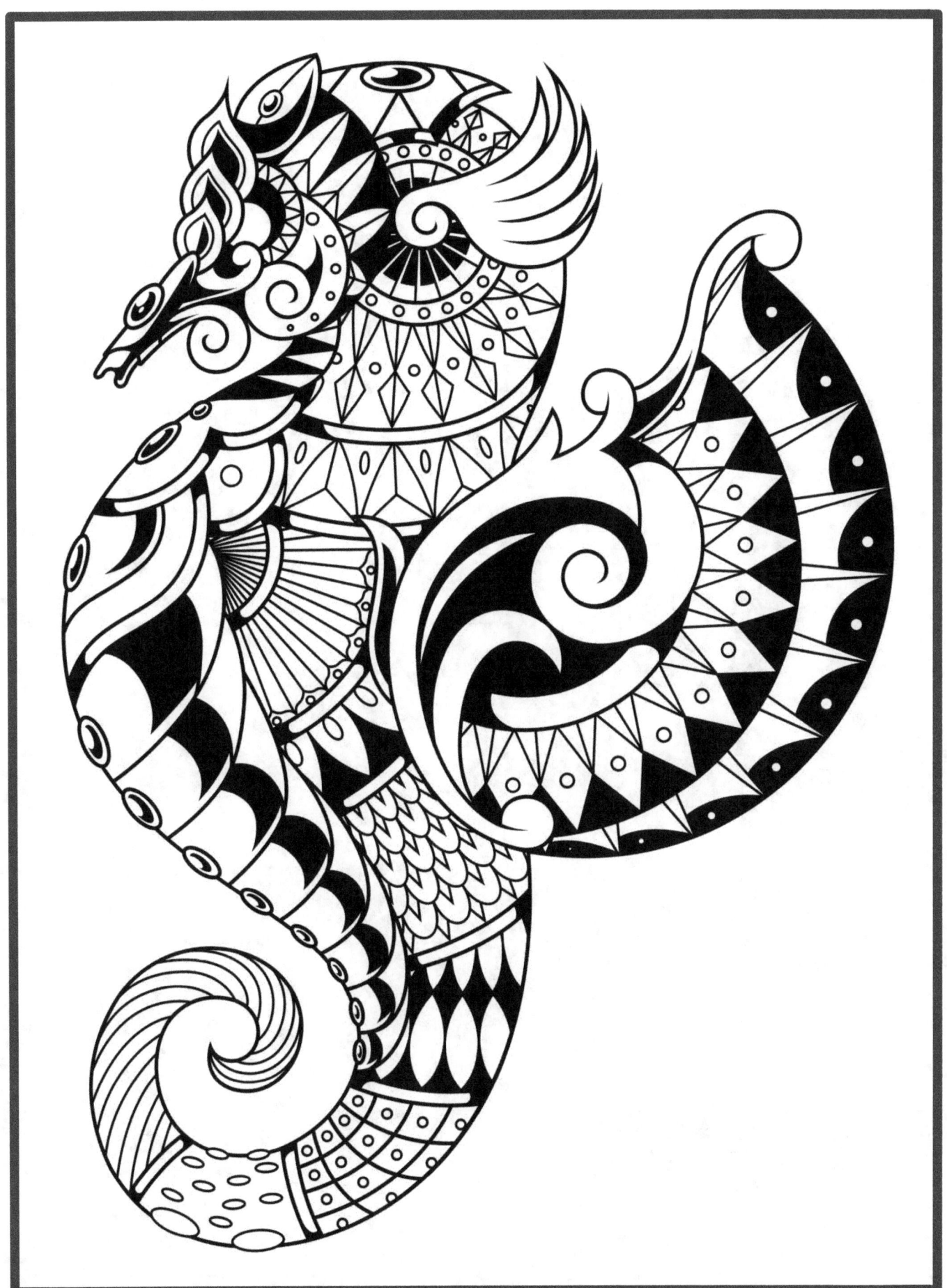

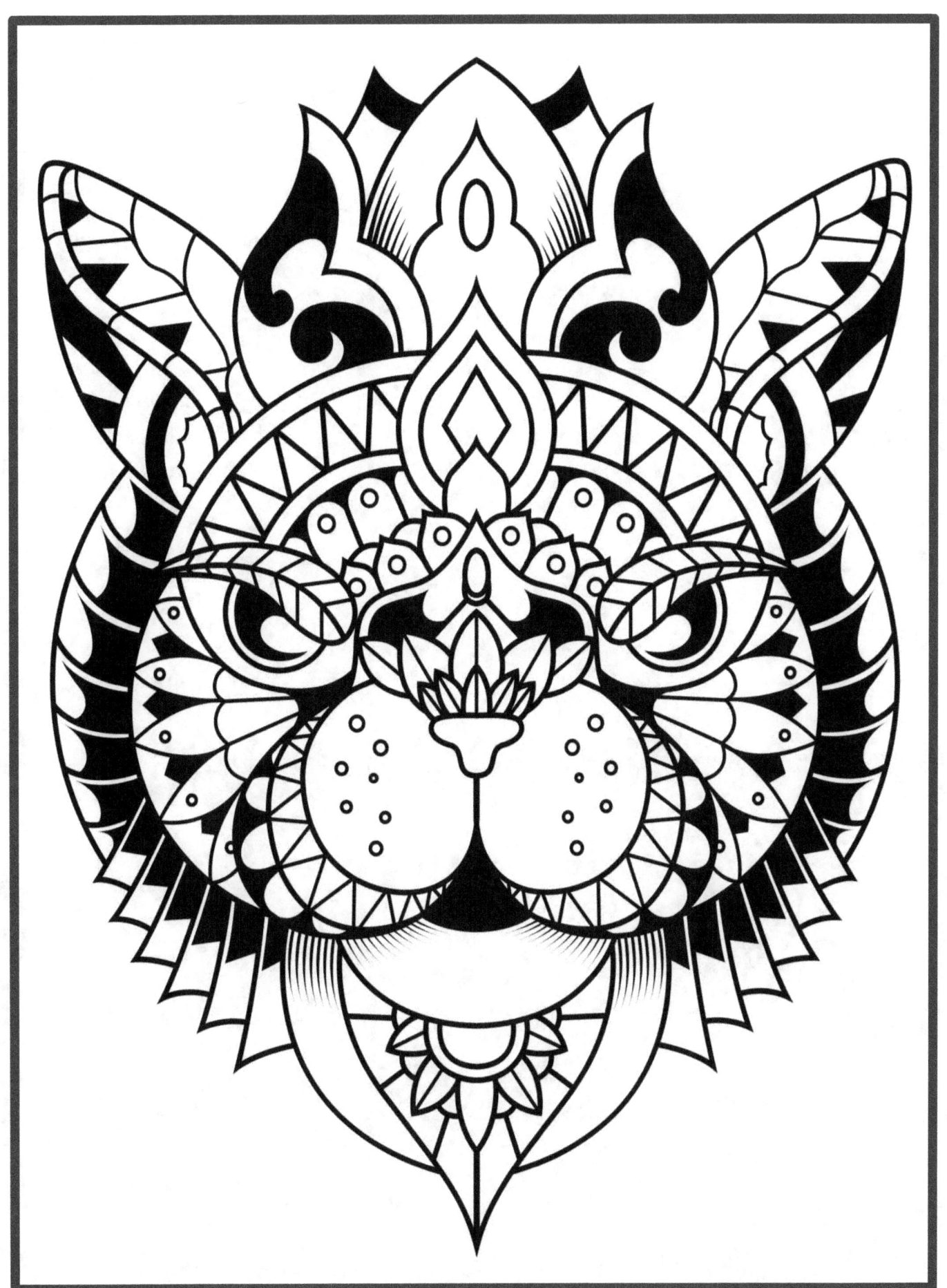

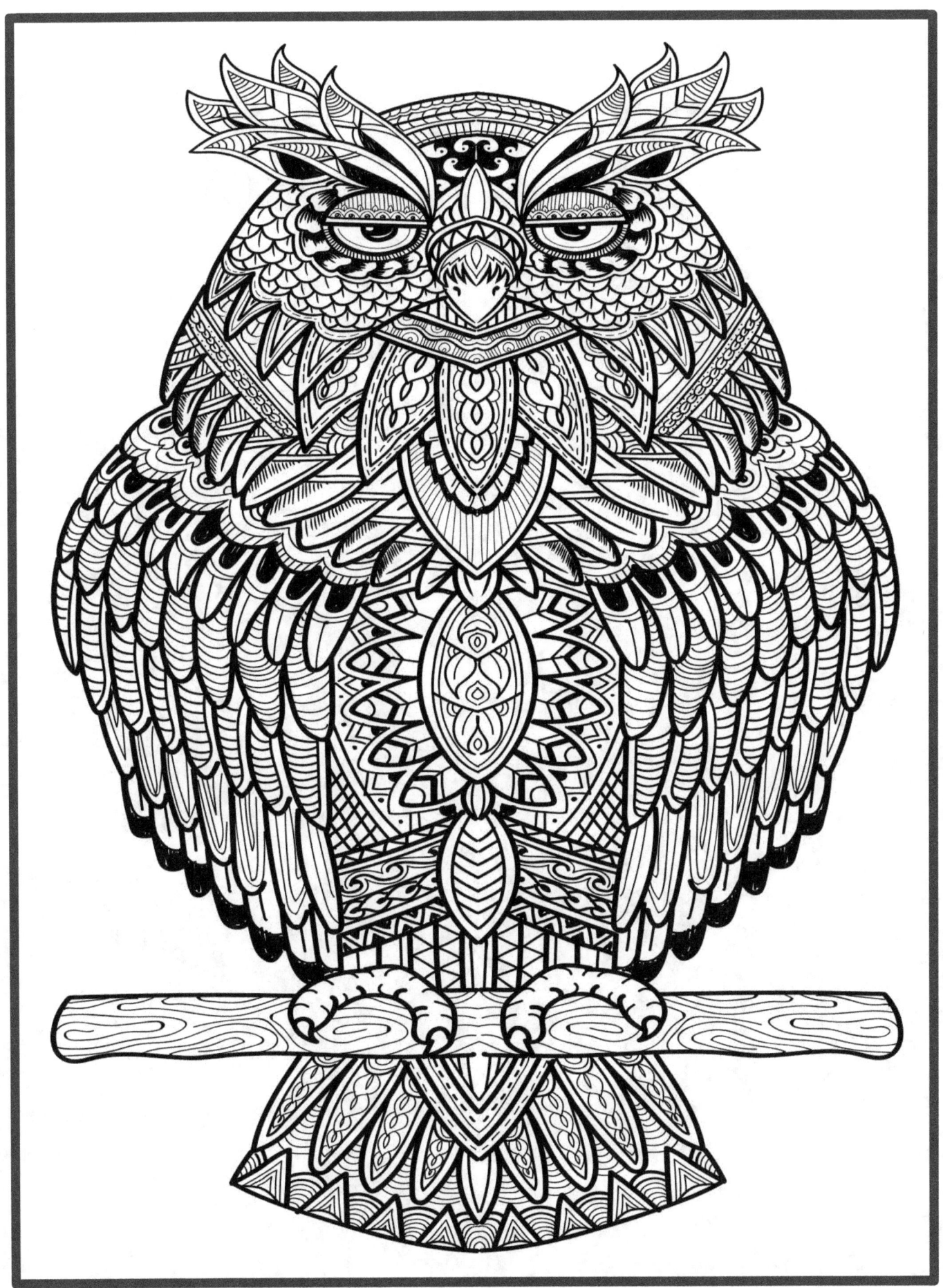

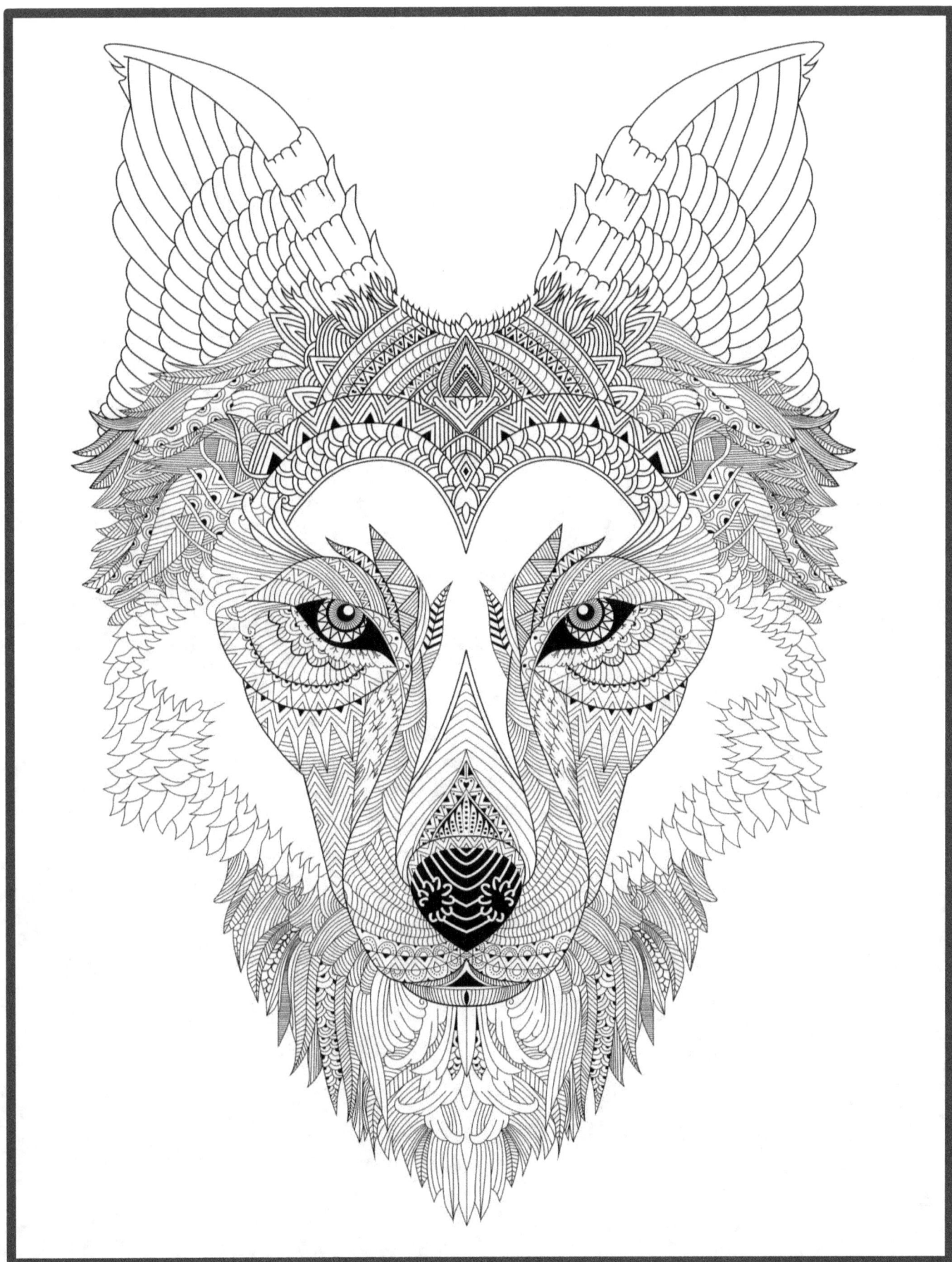

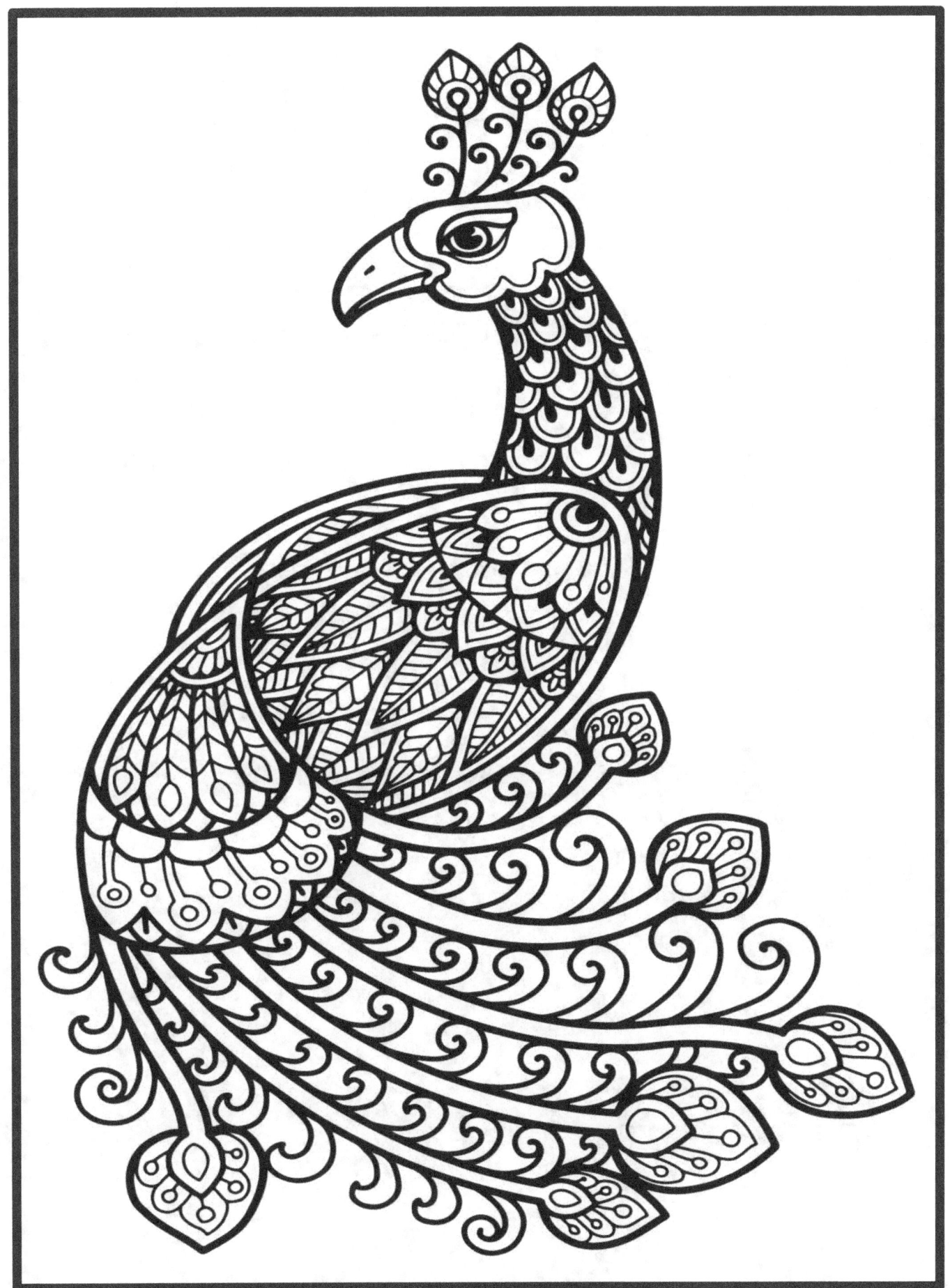

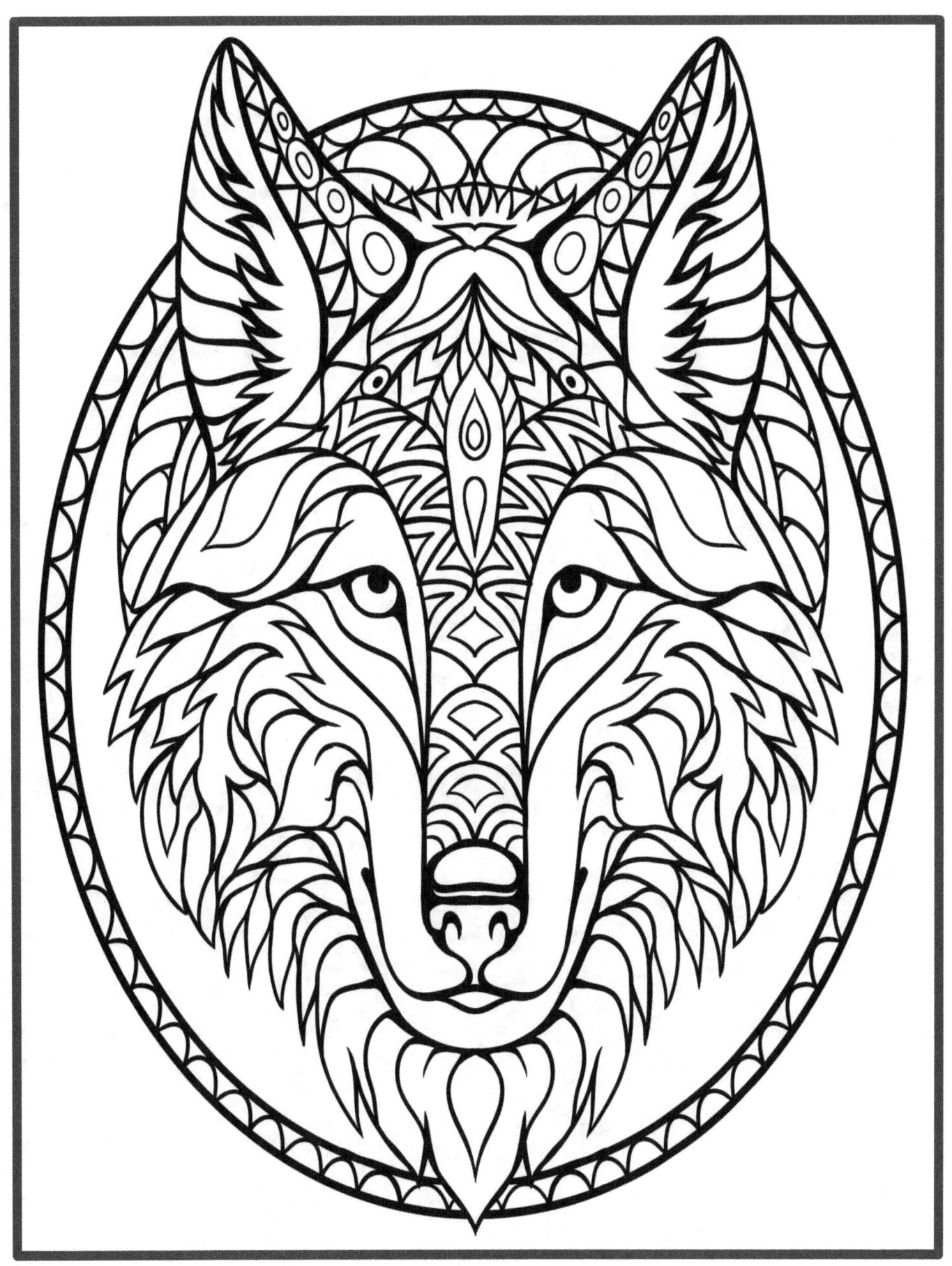

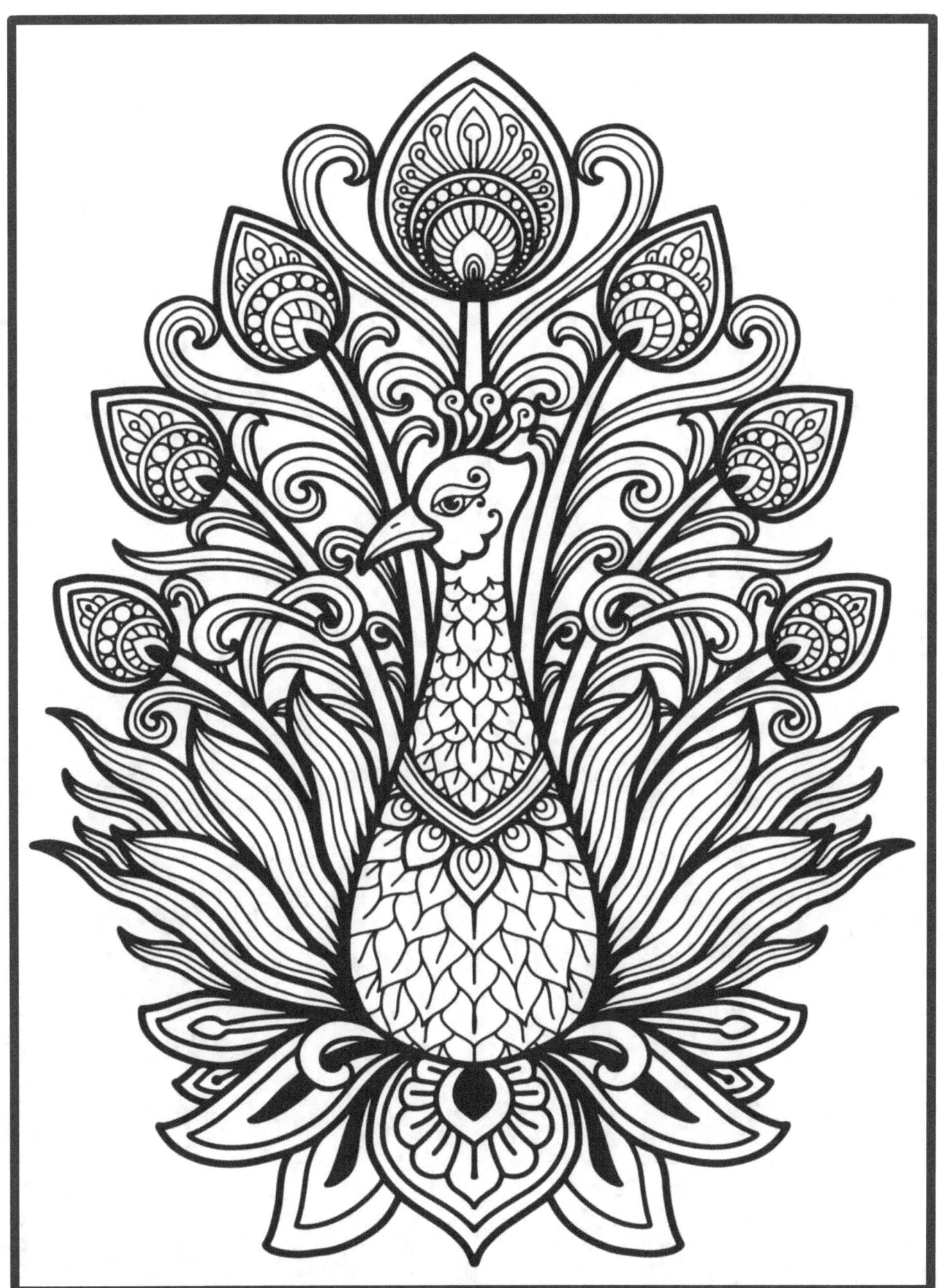

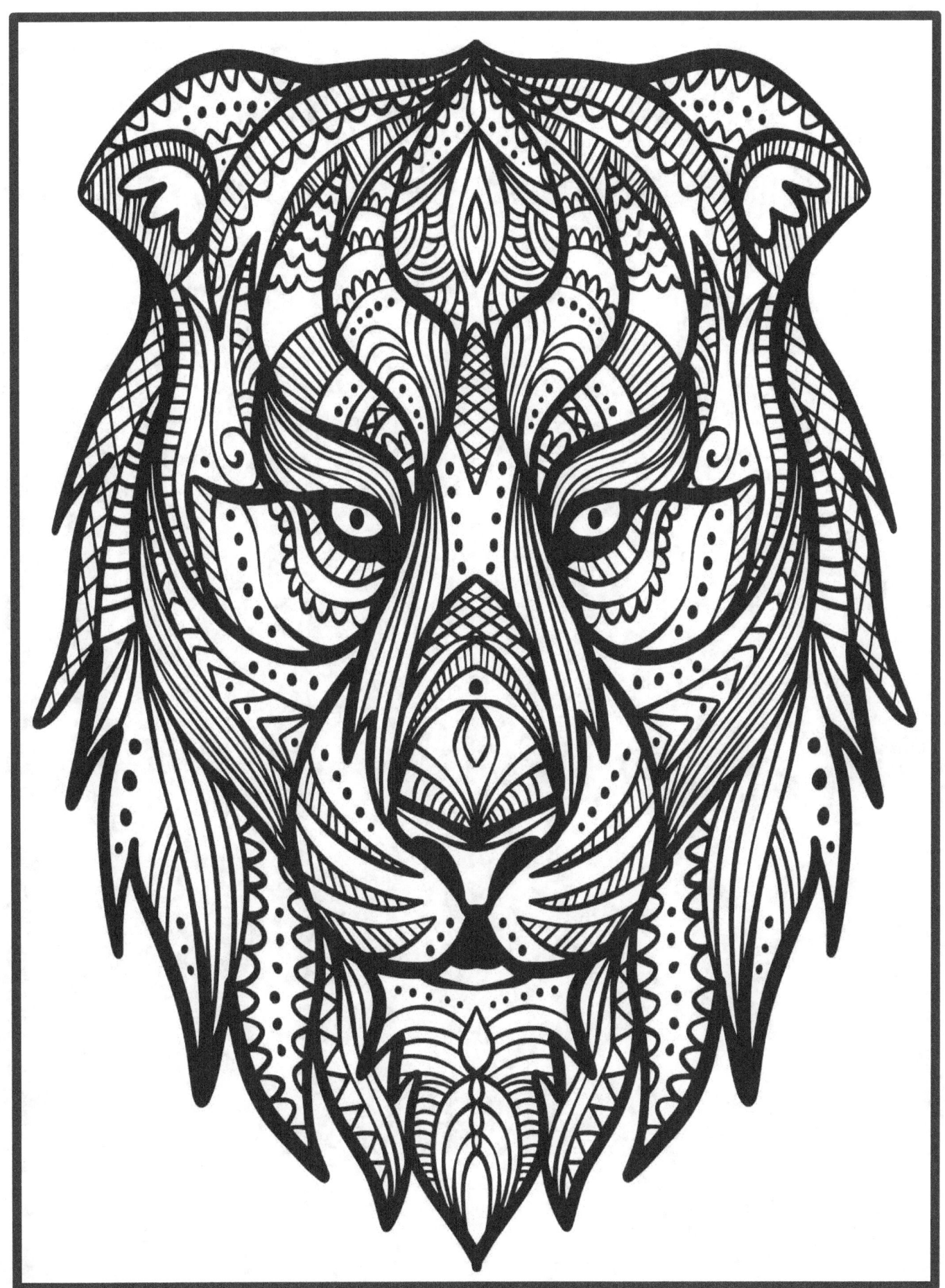

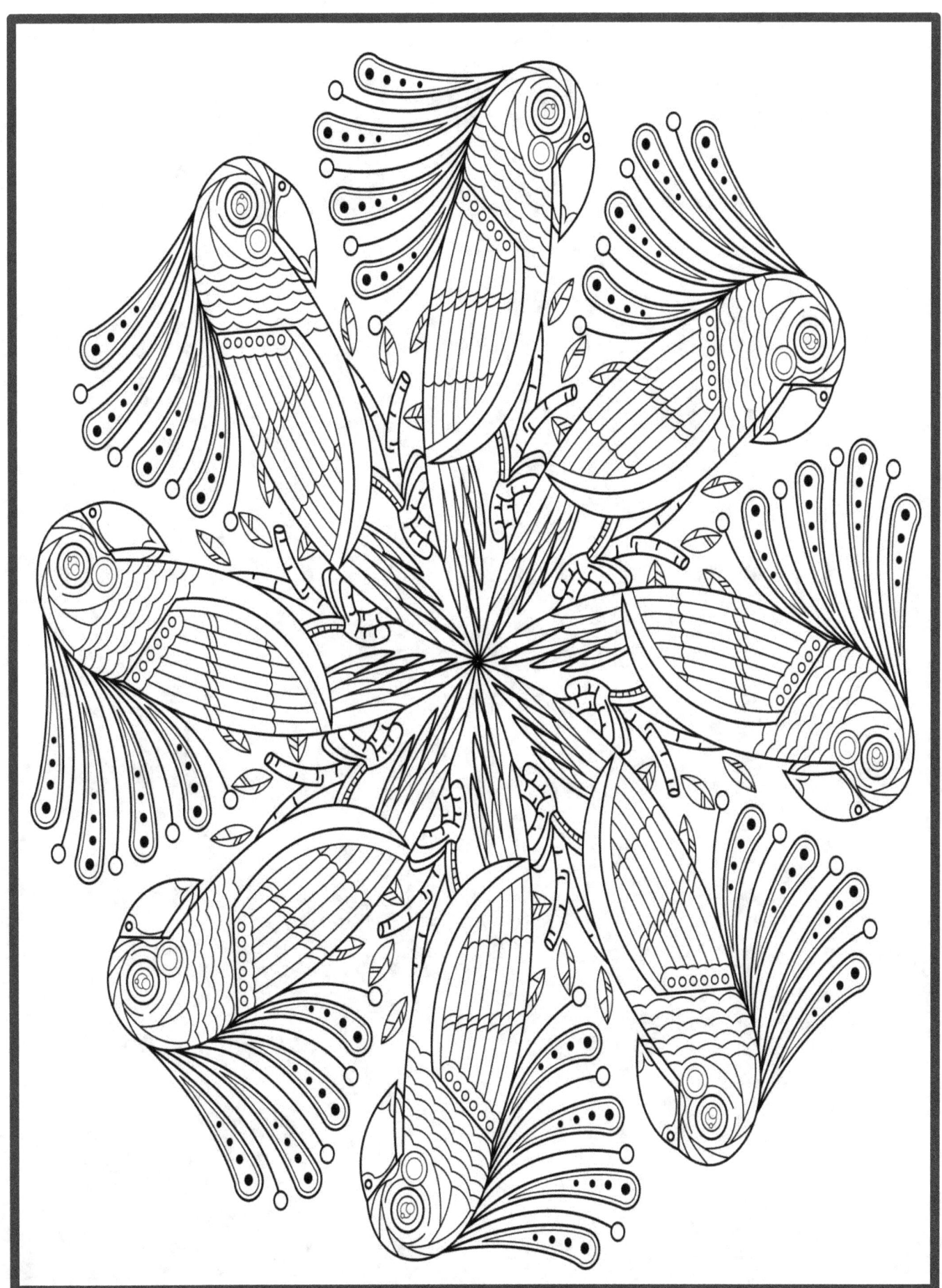

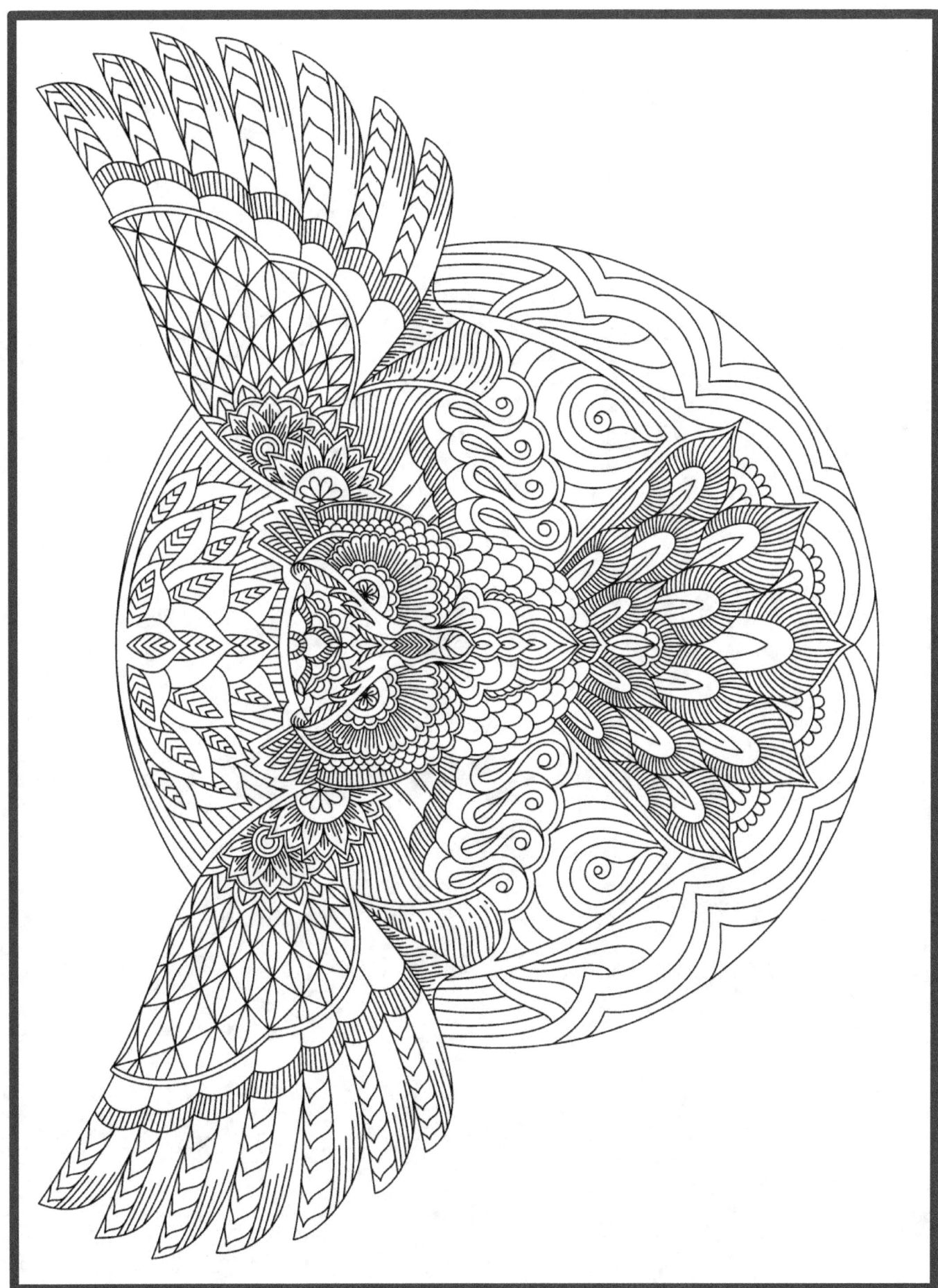

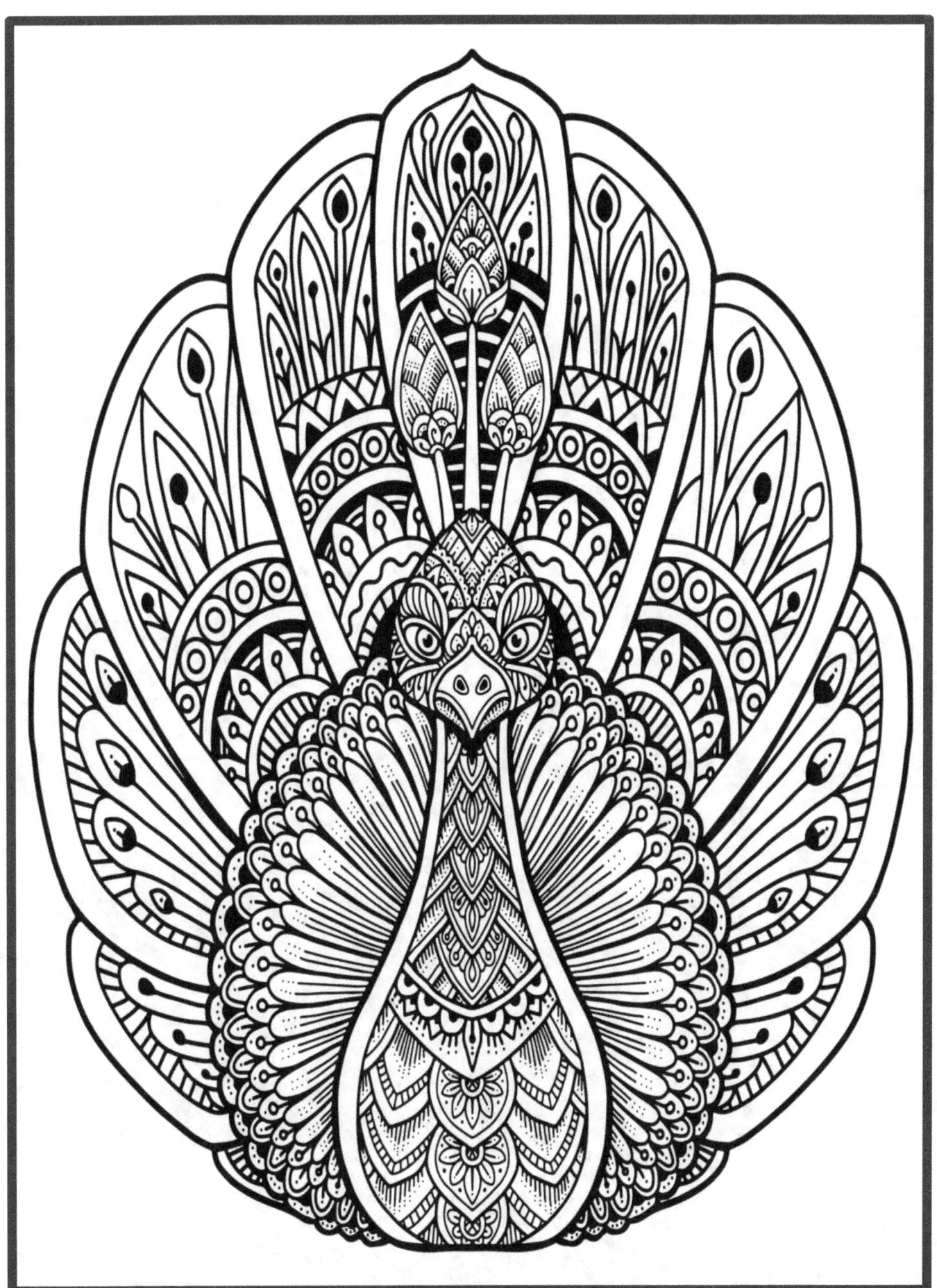

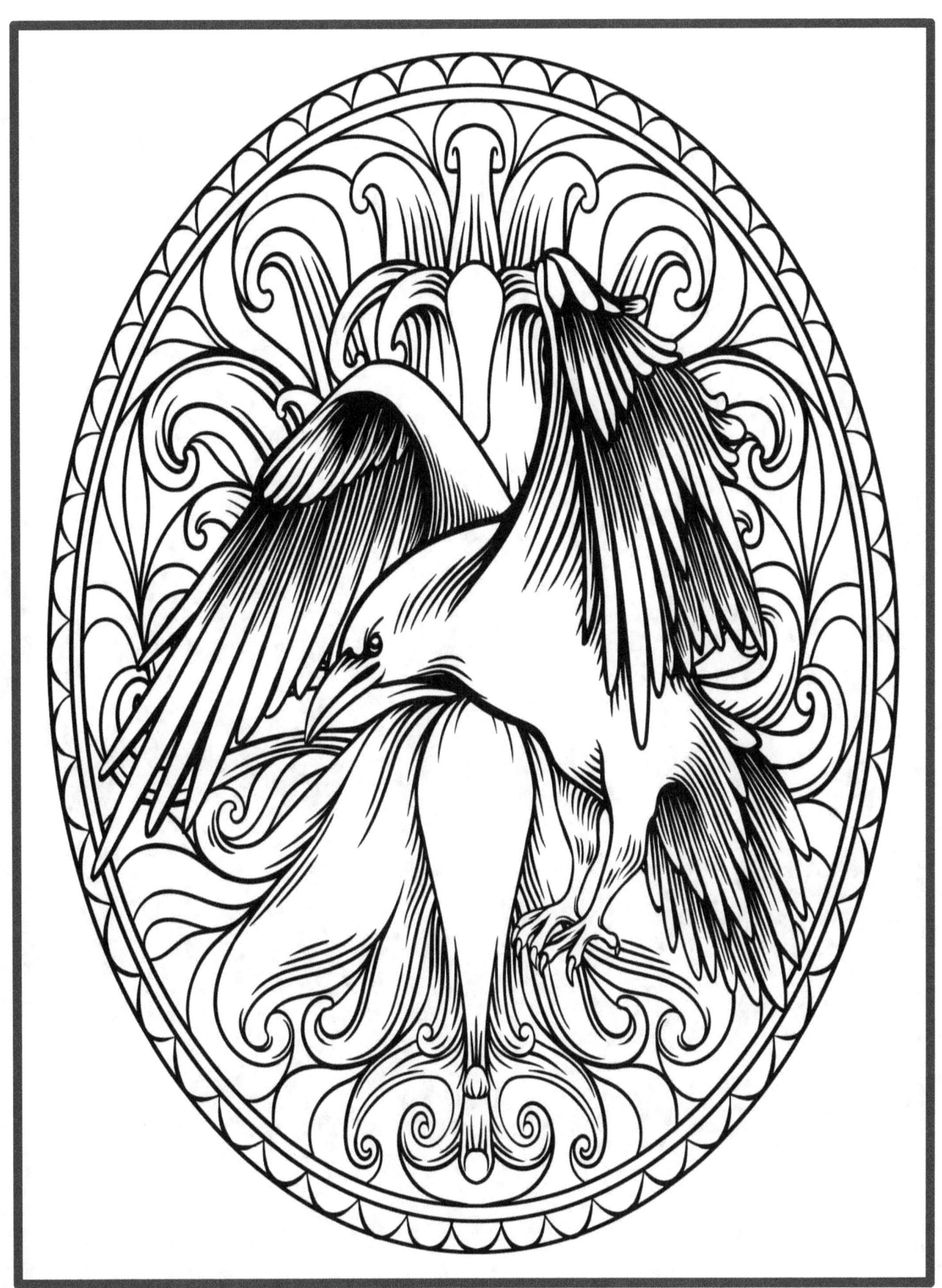

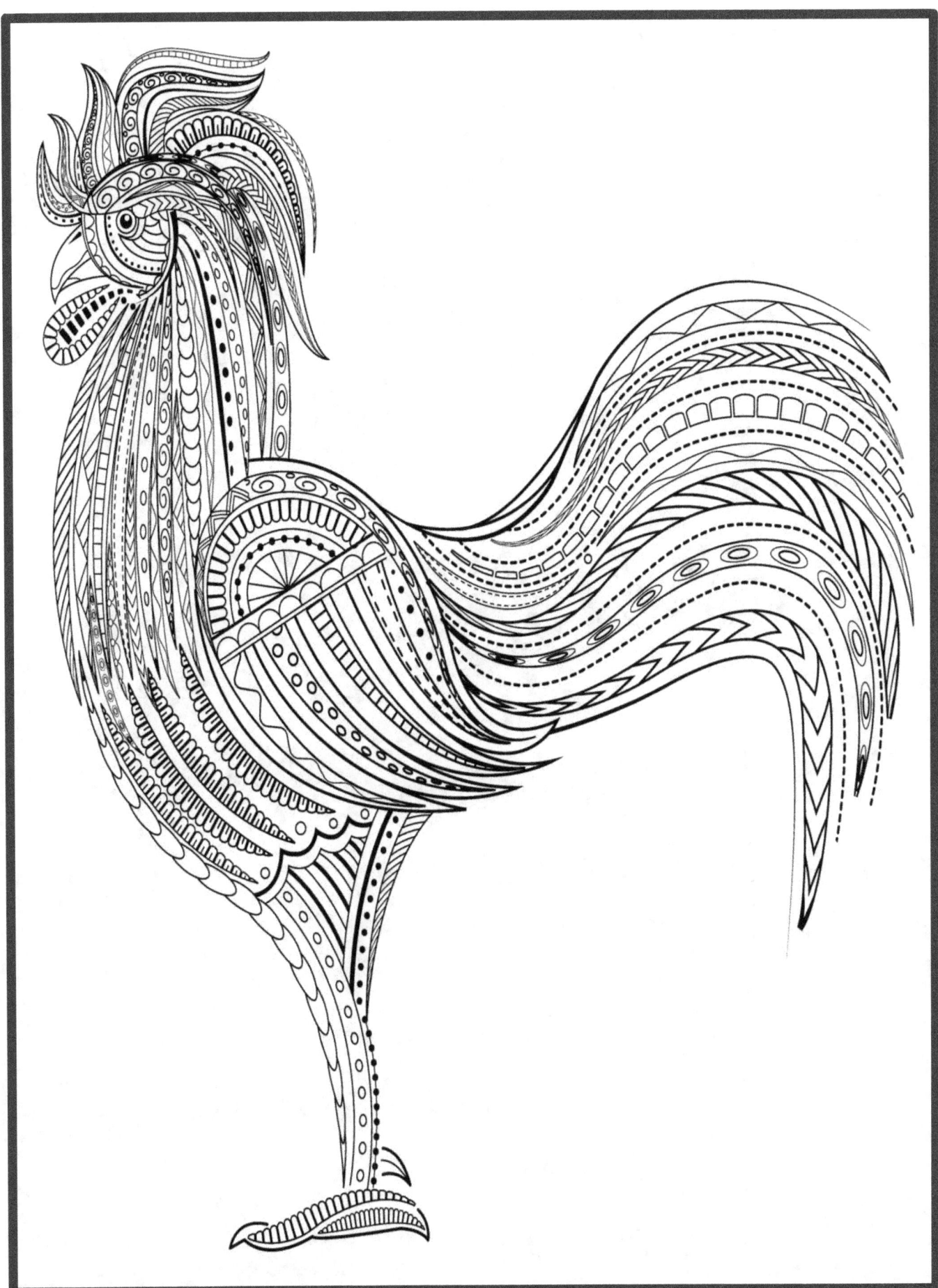

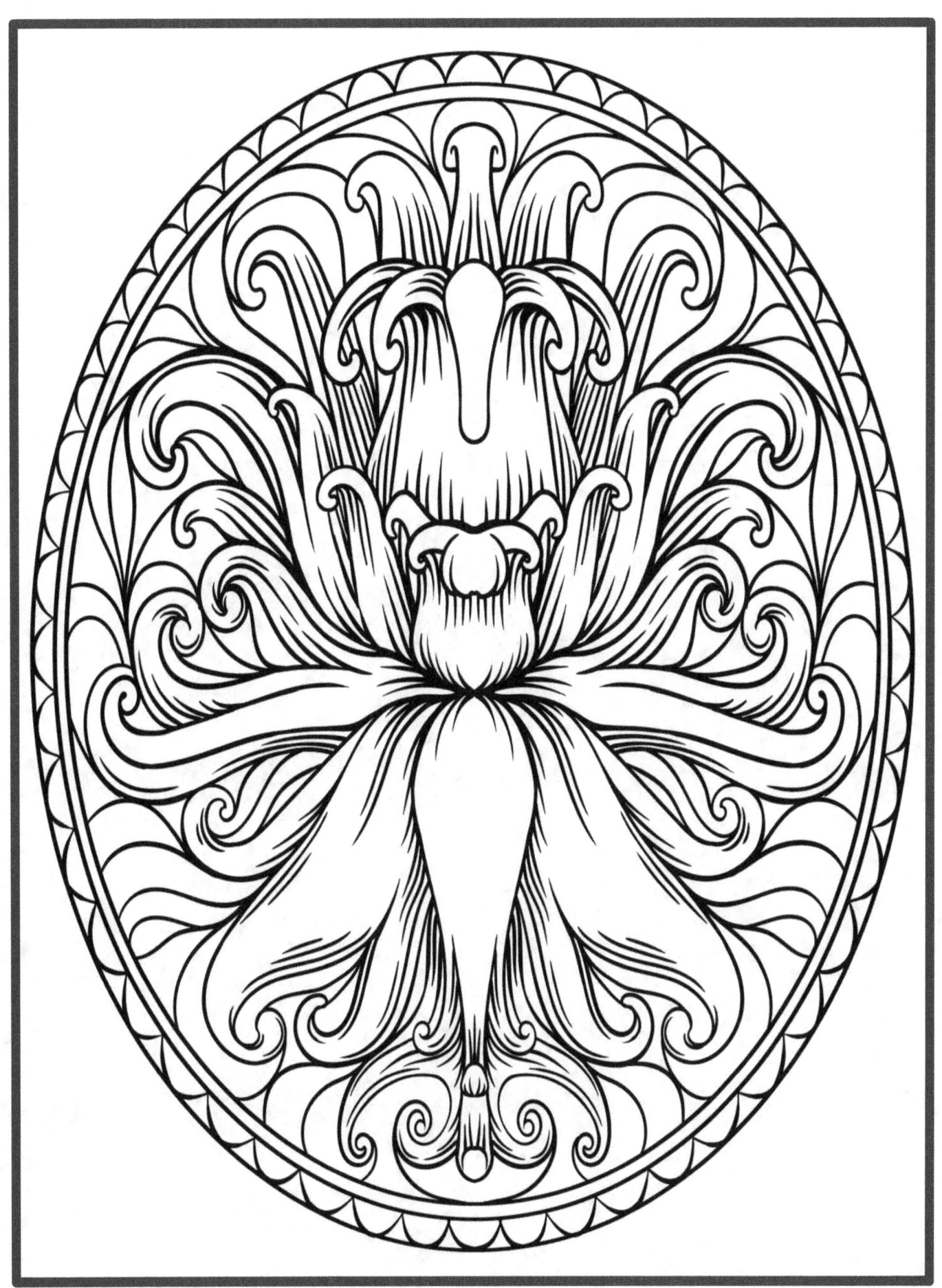

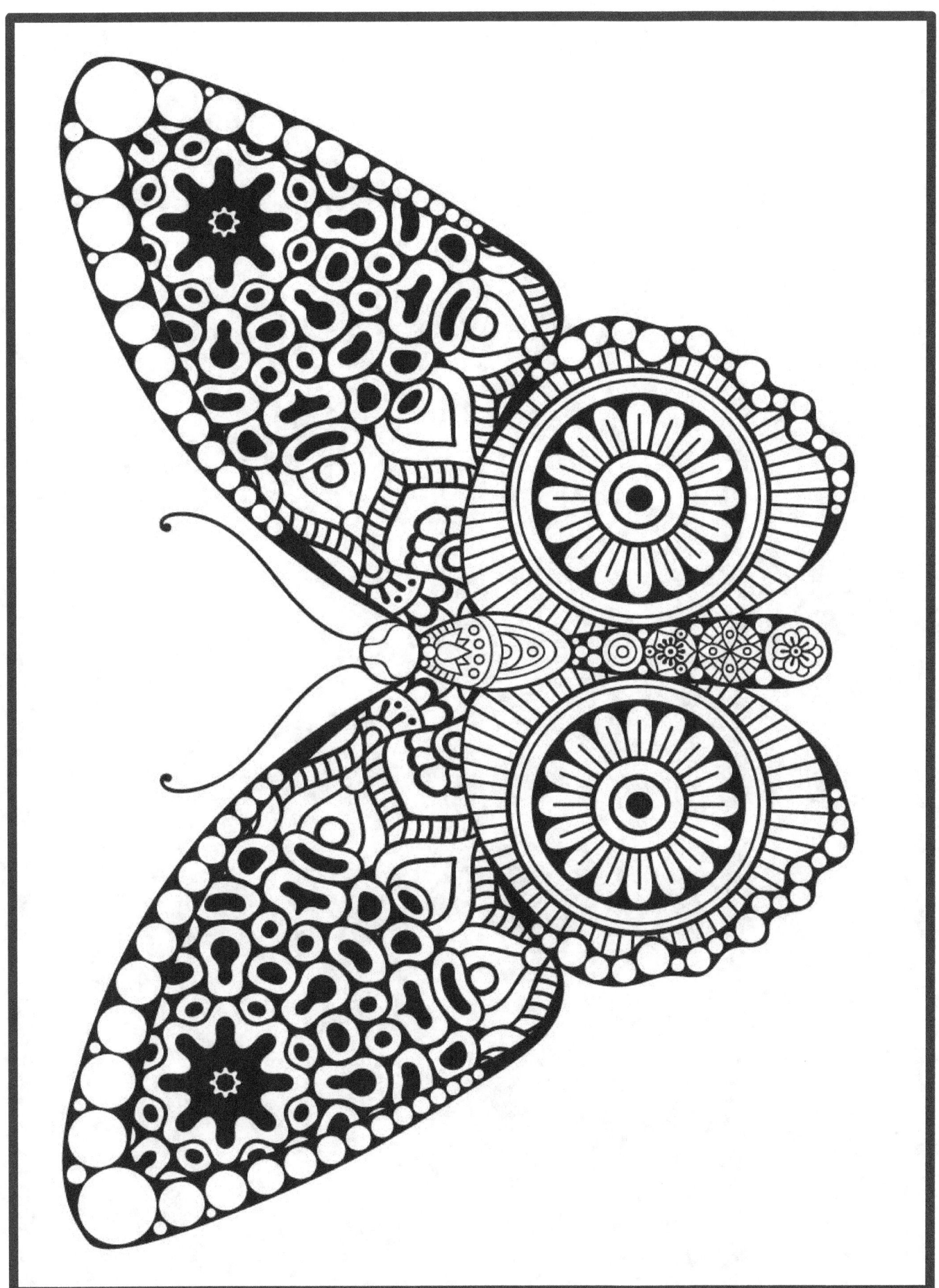

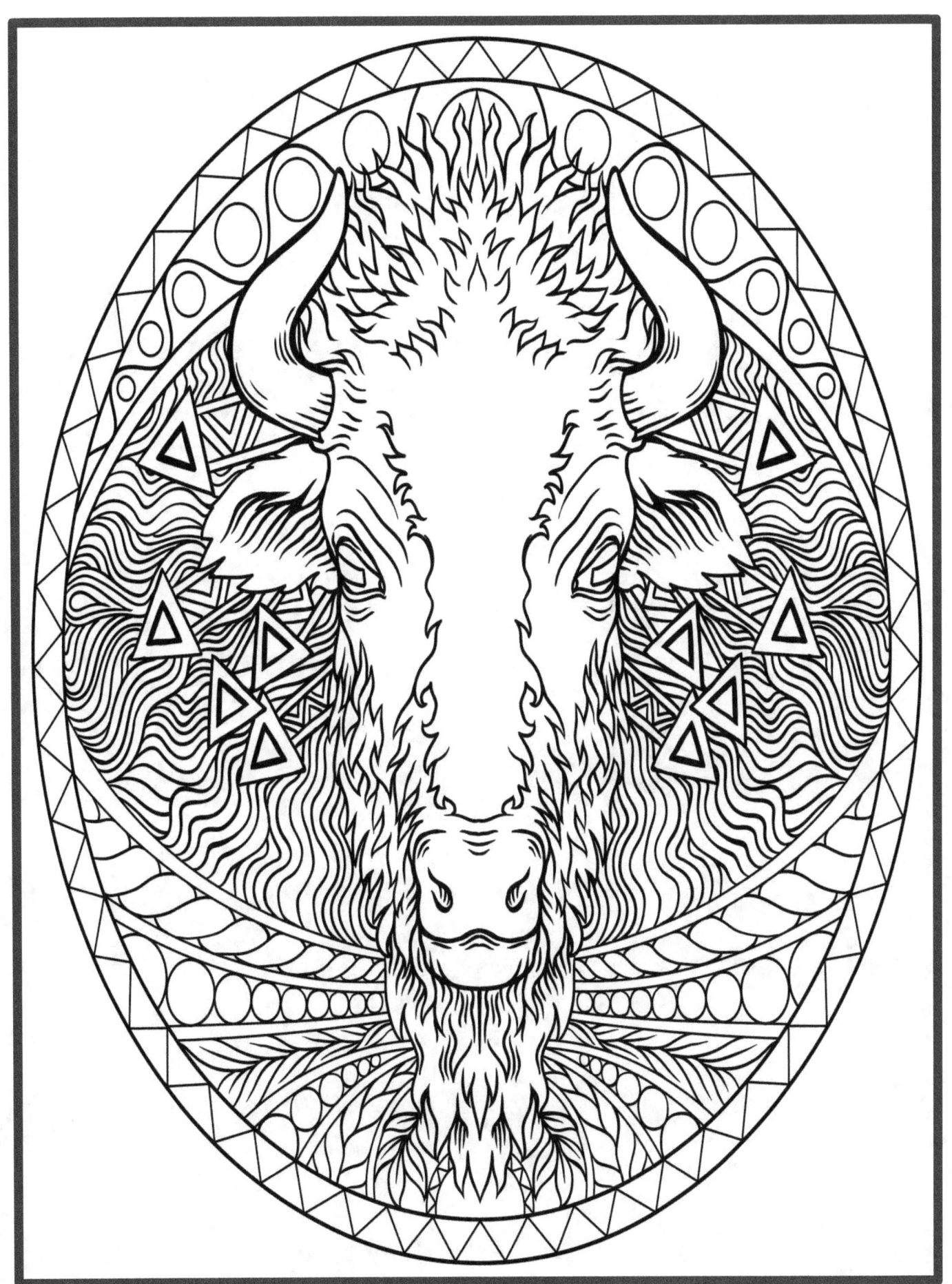

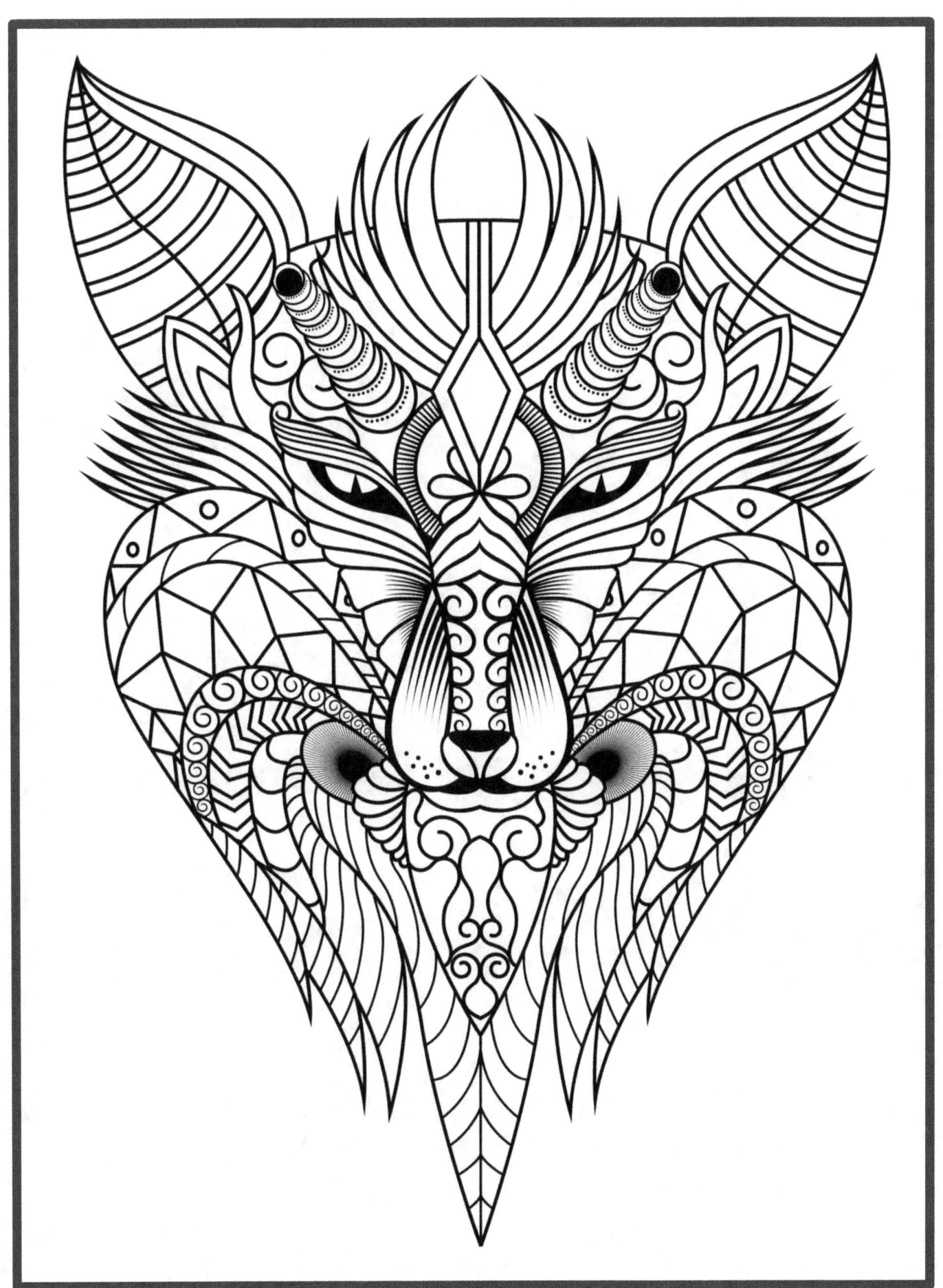

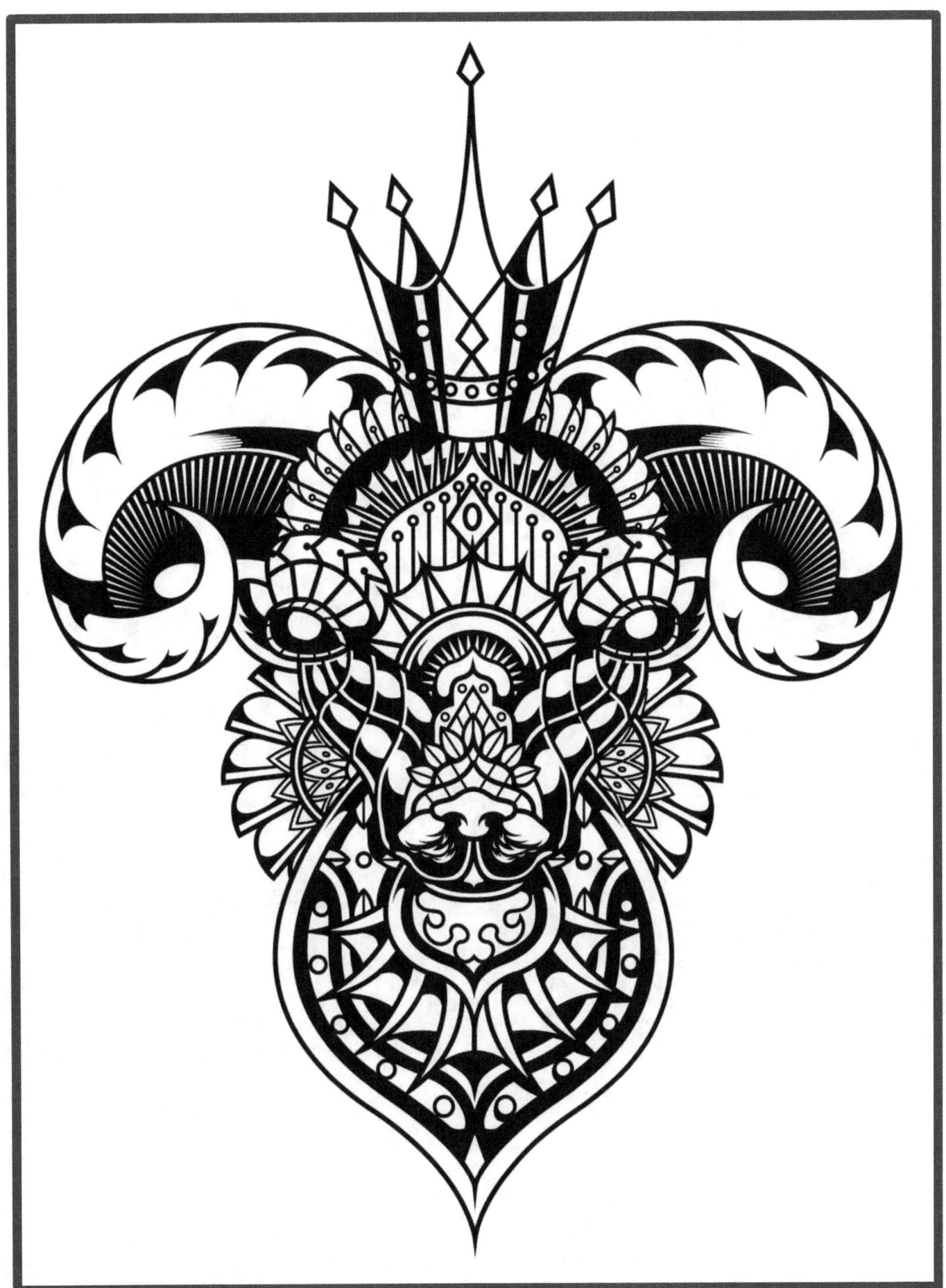

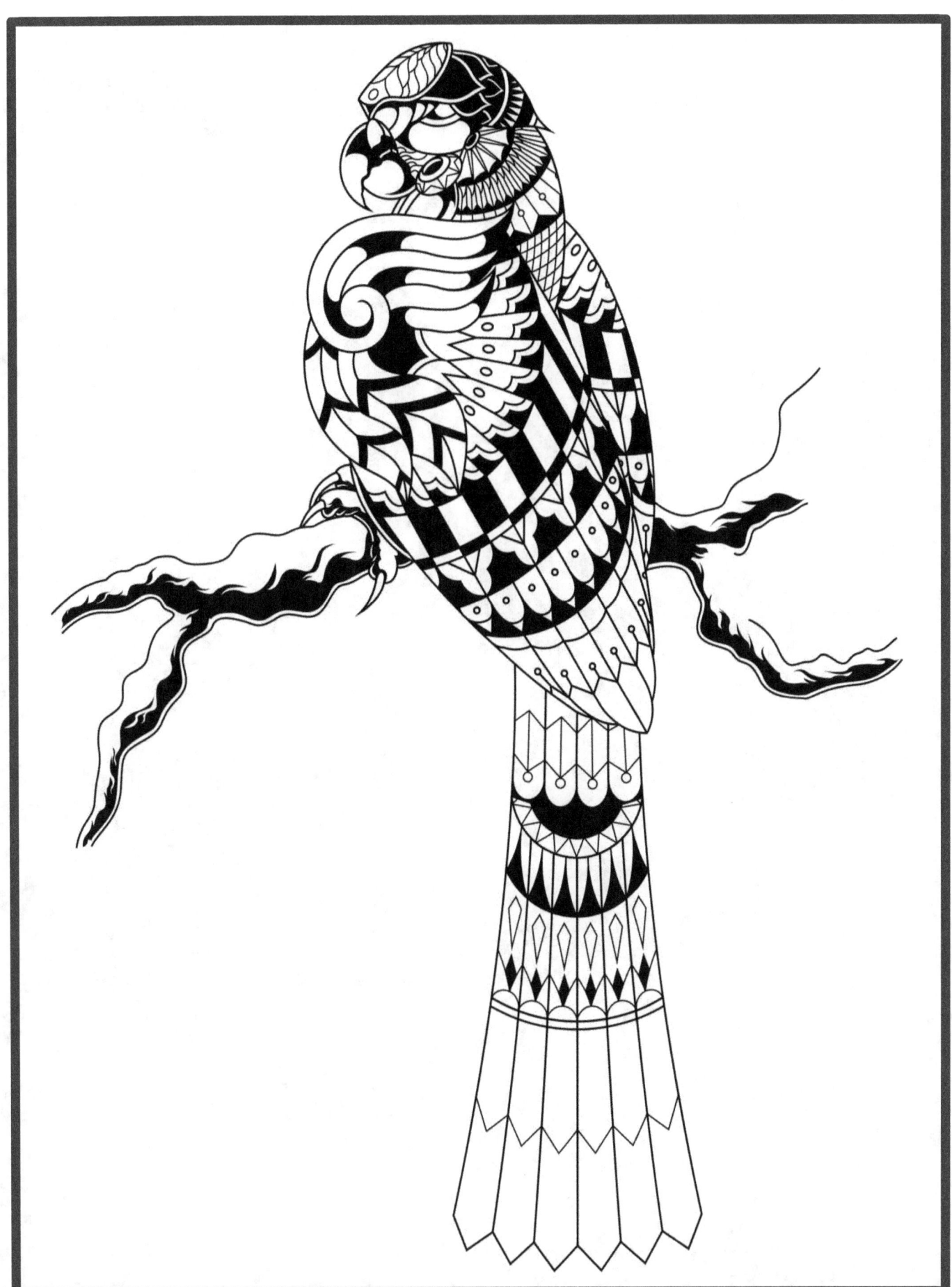

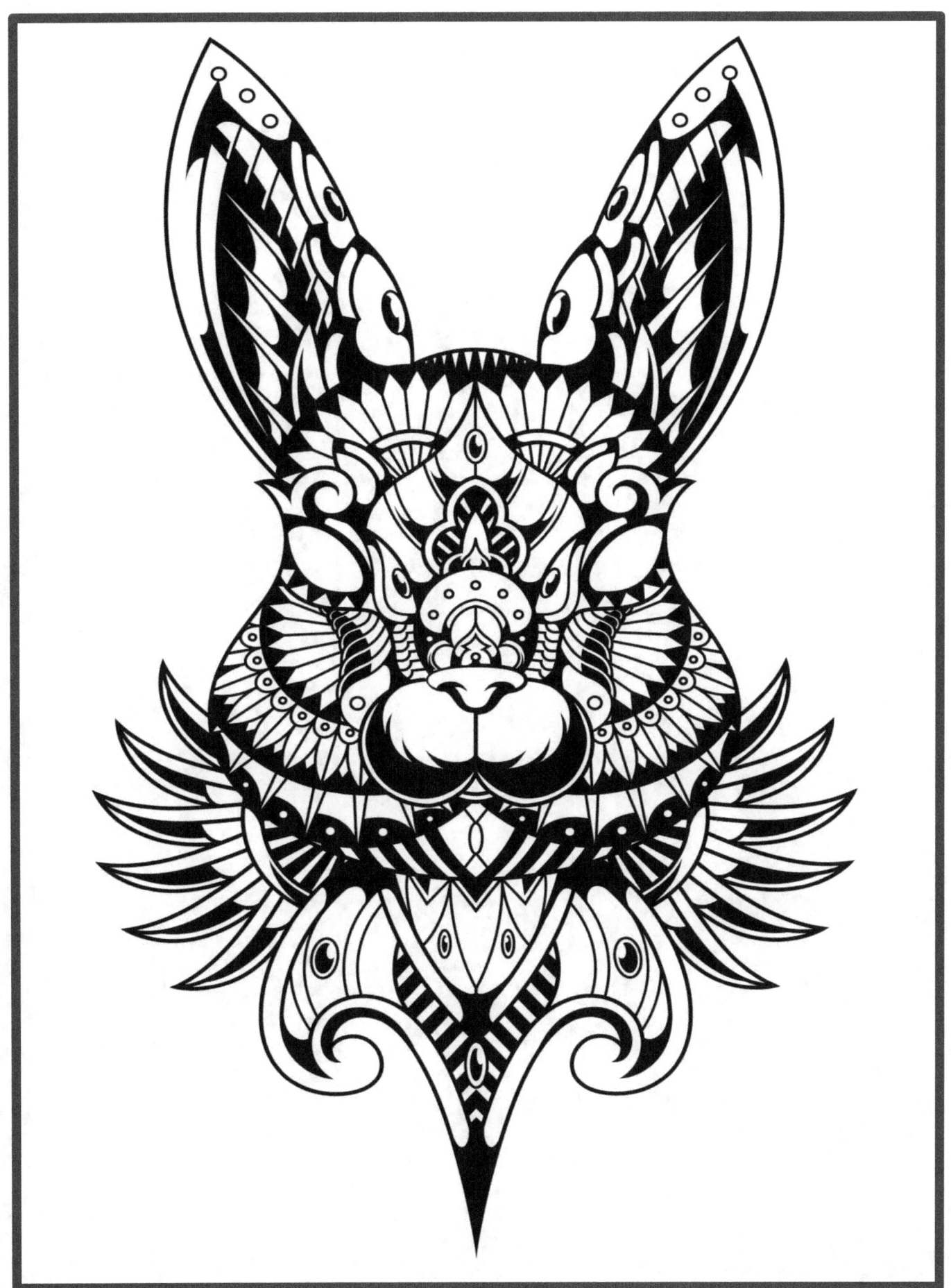

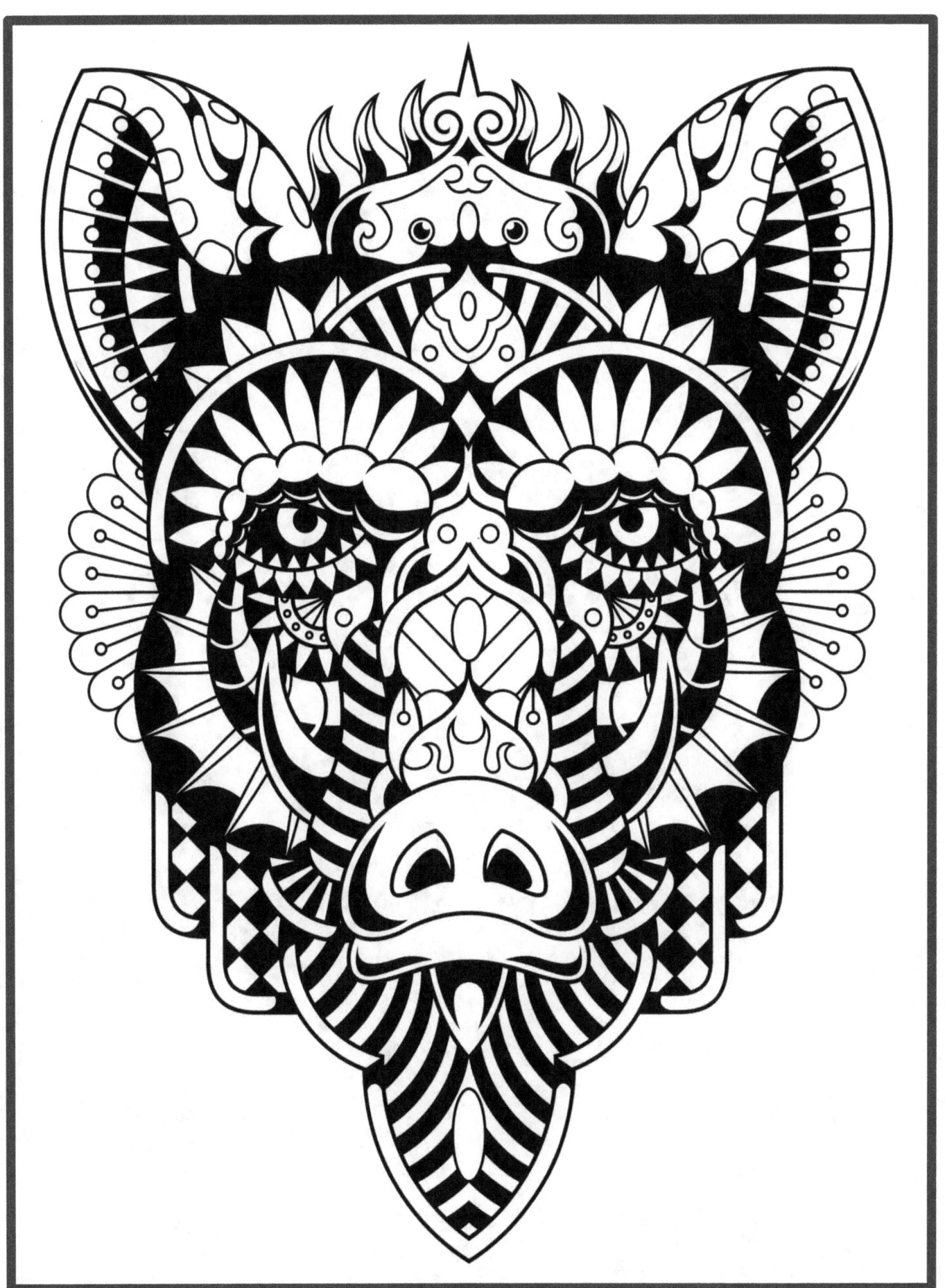

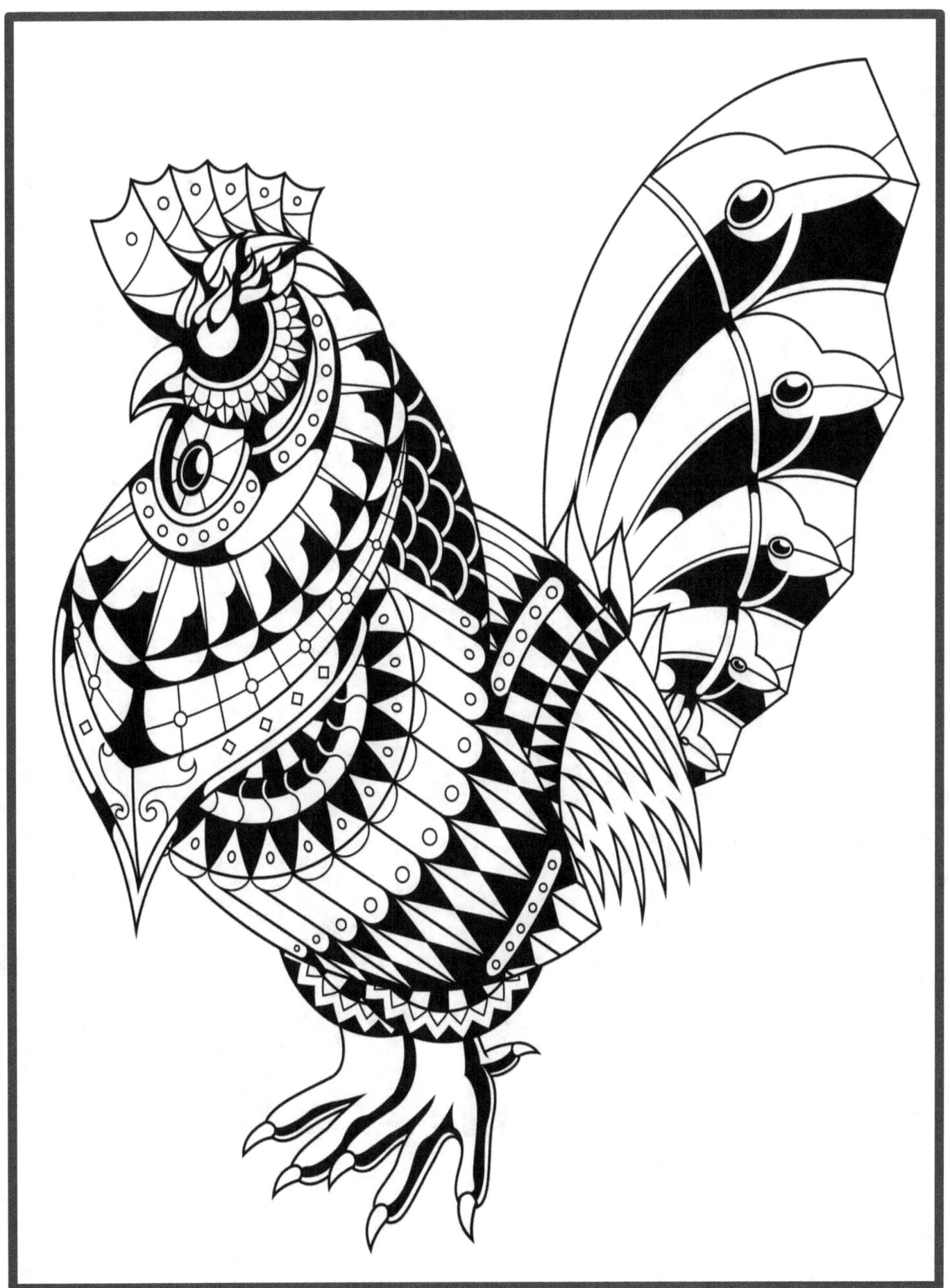

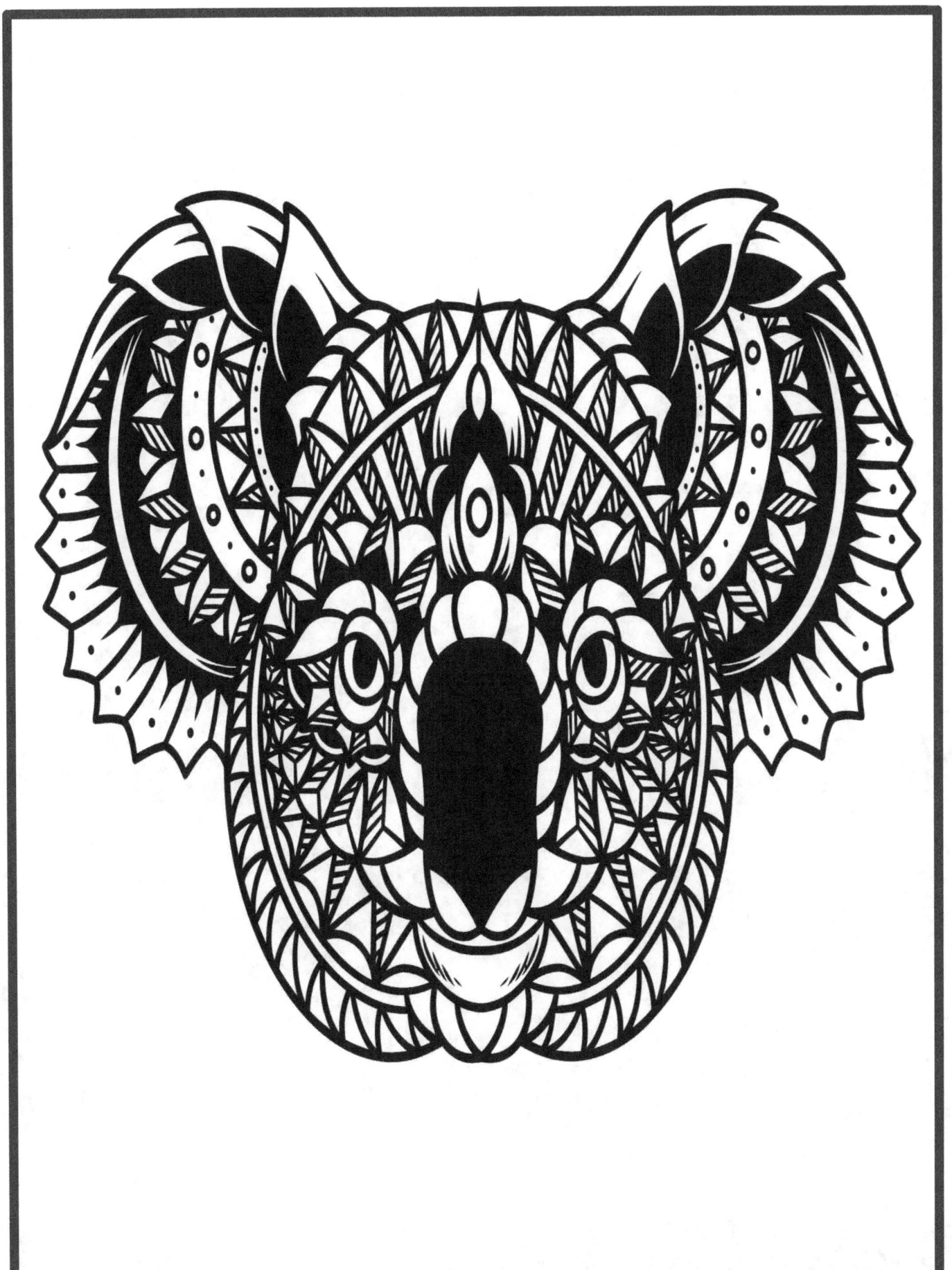

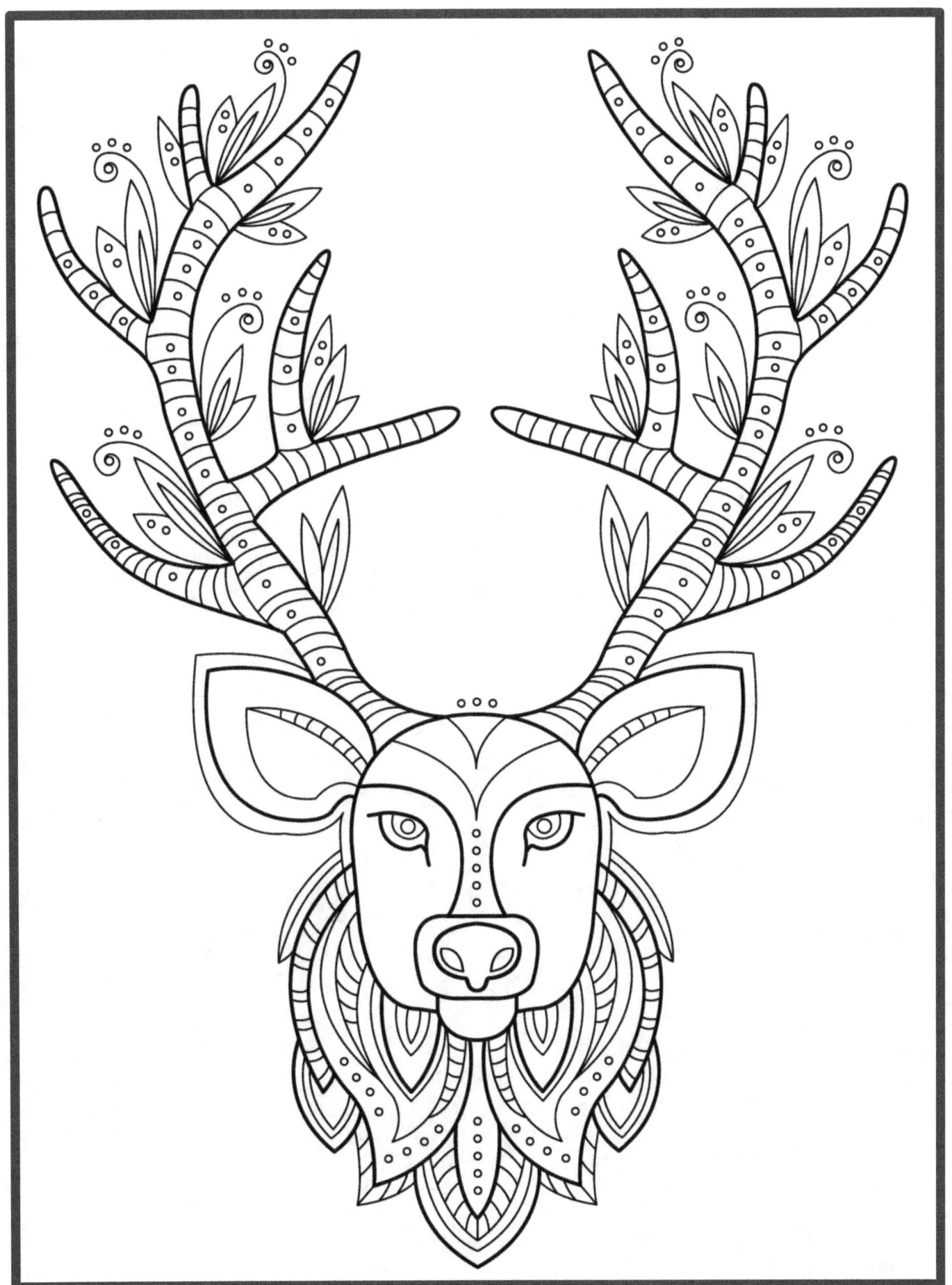

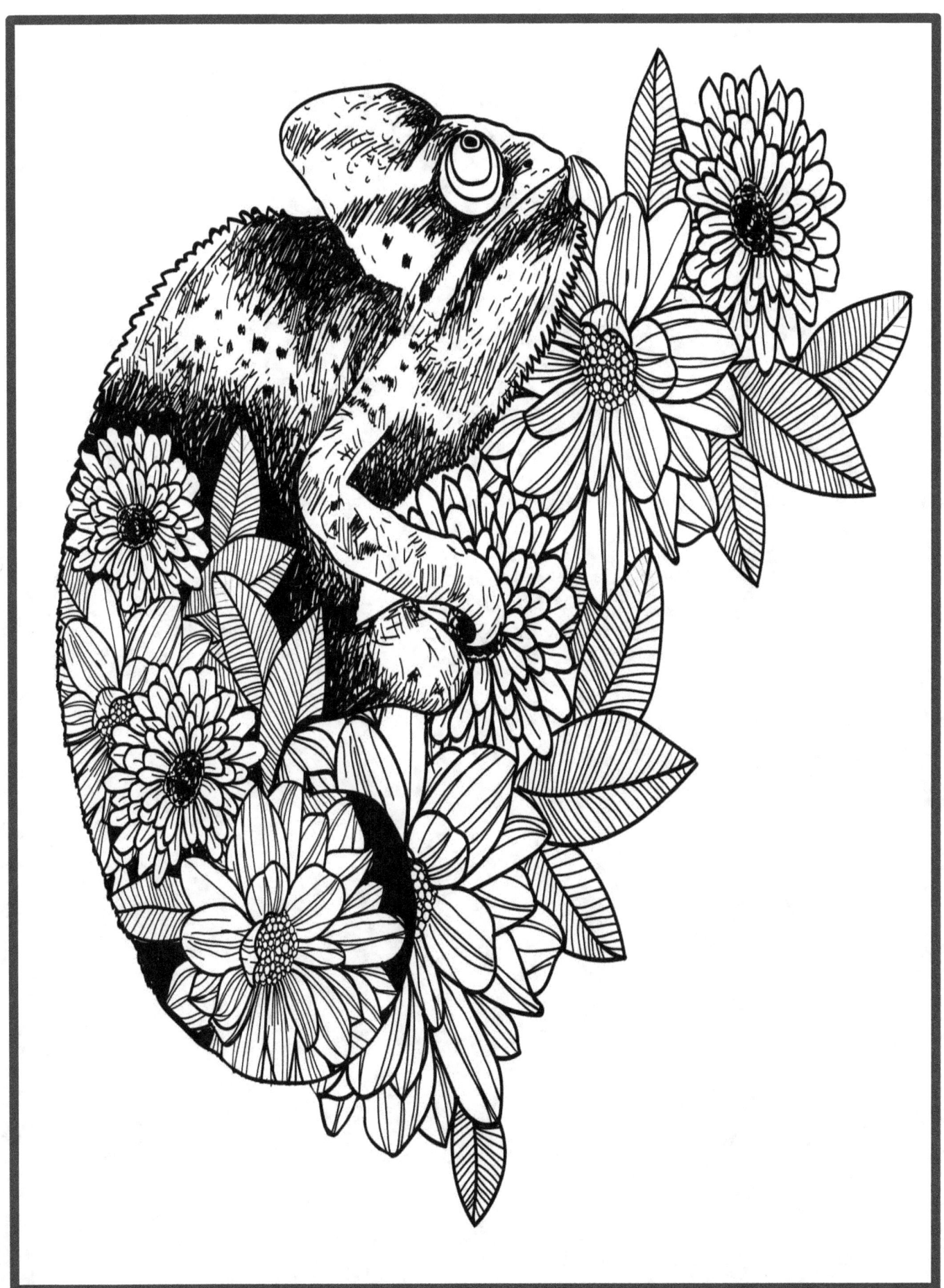

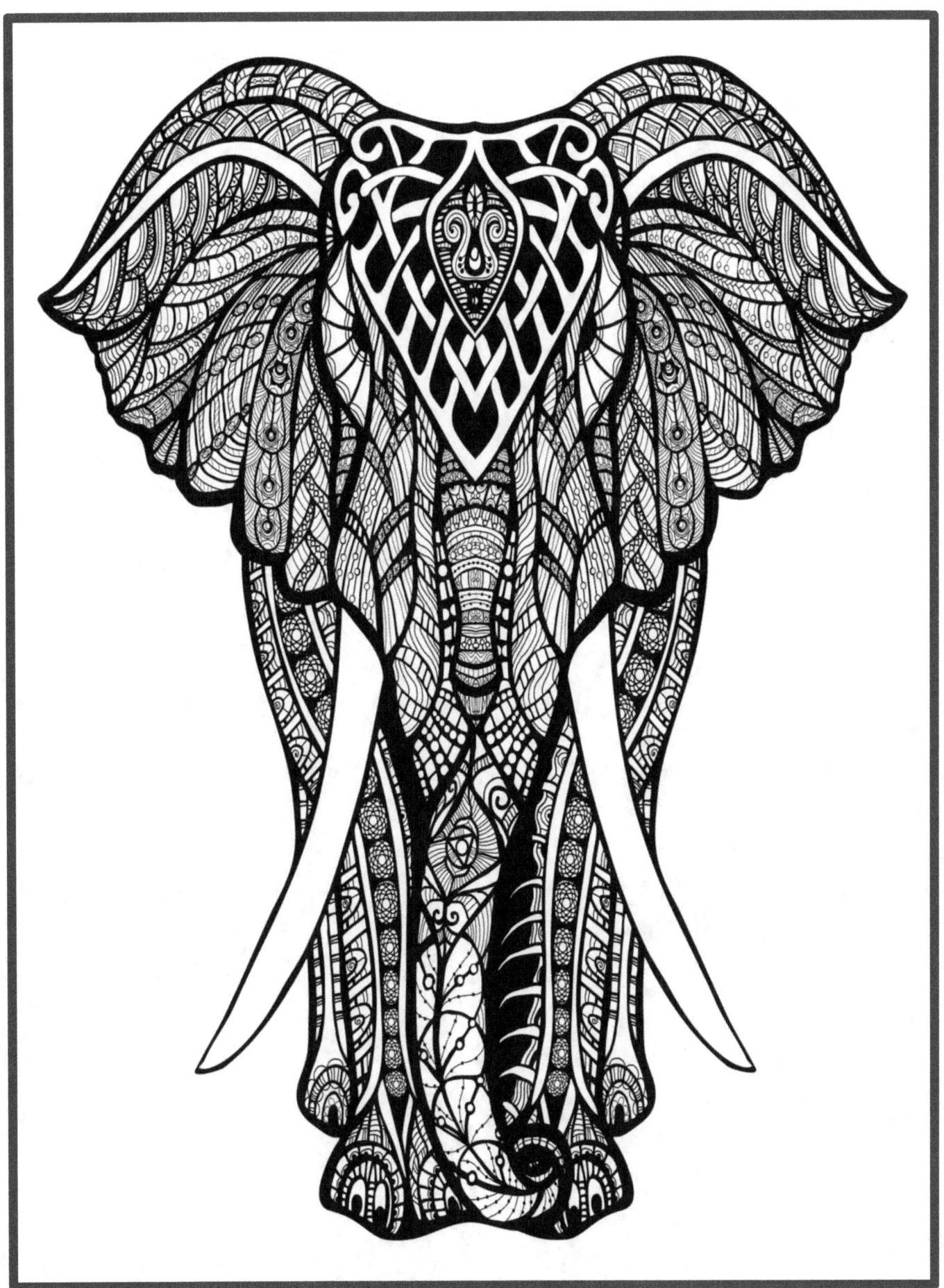

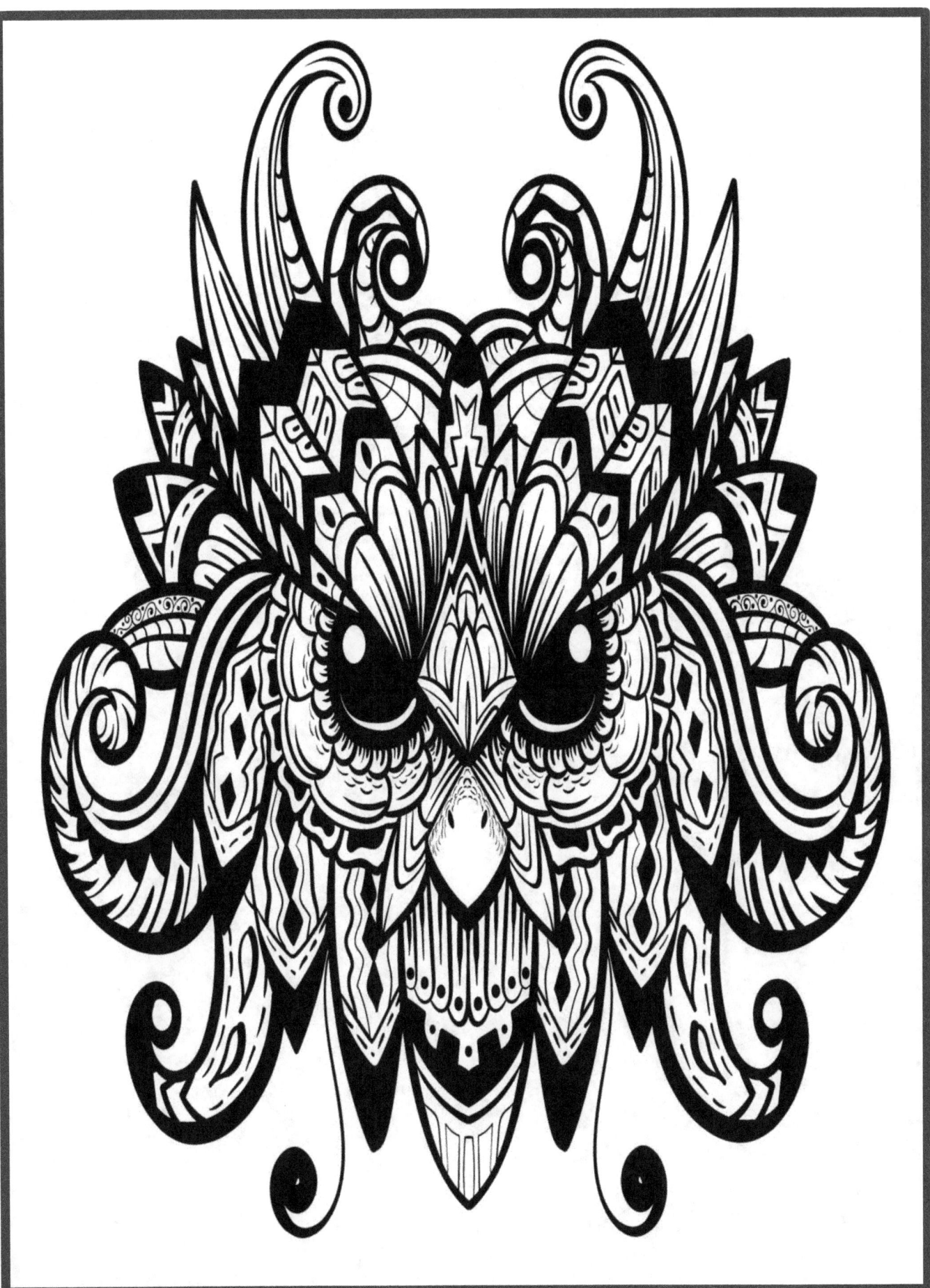

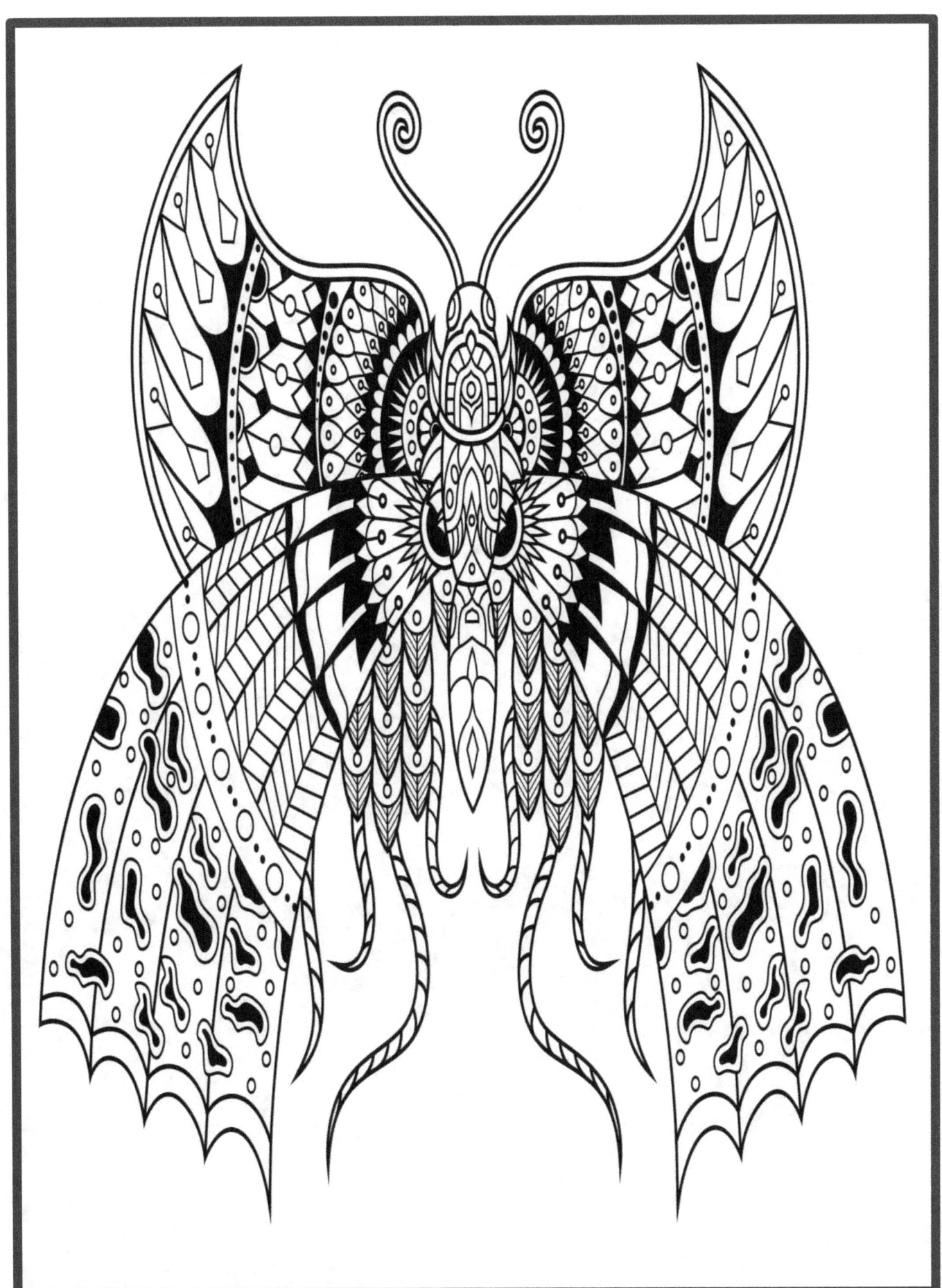

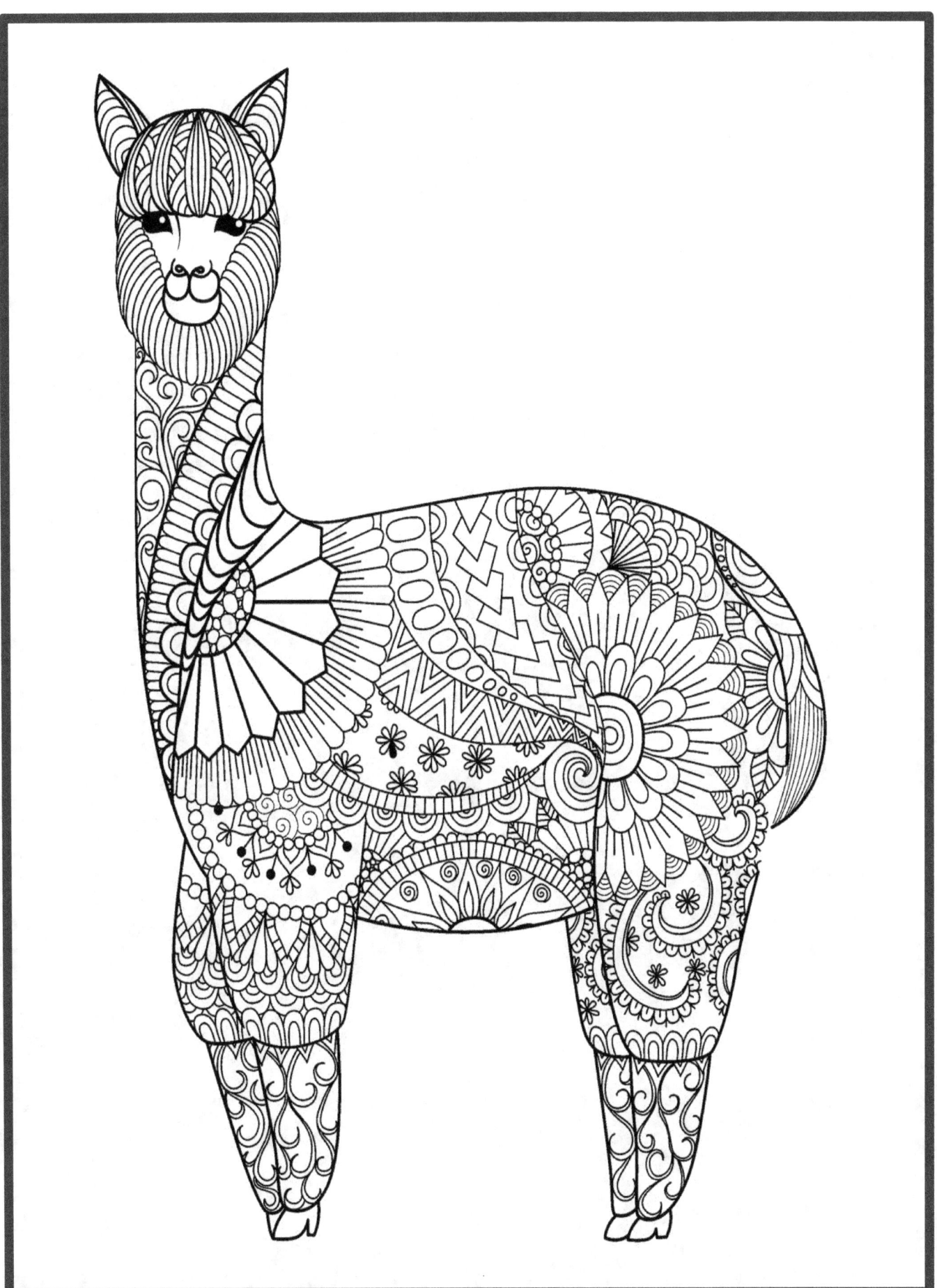

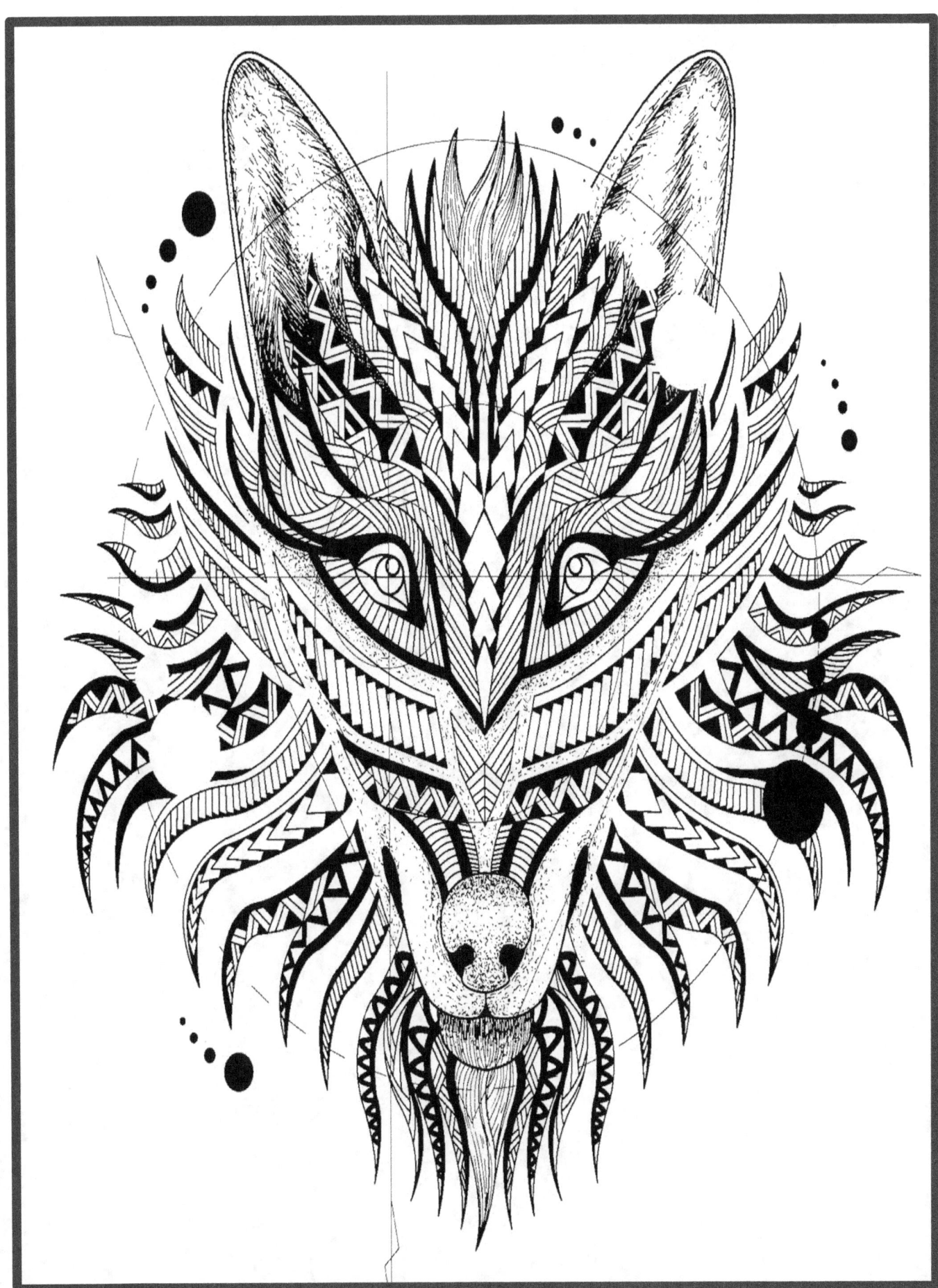

www.ingramcontent.com/pod-product-compliance
Lightning Source LLC
Chambersburg PA
CBHW060423220526
45465CB00008B/2995